LIFE IN ACTION

LIFE IN

JEREMY P. TARCHER/PENGUIN

a member of Penguin Group (USA) Inc.

ACTION

The 12 VOY Principles of
True Happiness and Success

FERNANDO ESPUELAS

Most Tarcher/Penguin books are available at special quantity discounts for bulk purchase for sales promotions, premiums, fund-raising, and educational needs. Special books or book excerpts also can be created to fit specific needs. For details, write Penguin Group (USA) Inc. Special Markets, 375 Hudson Street, New York, NY 10014.

Jeremy P. Tarcher/Penguin
a member of
Penguin Group (USA) Inc.
375 Hudson Street
New York, NY 10014
www.penguin.com

Library of Congress Cataloging-in-Publication Data

Espuelas, Fernando, date.
Life in action: the 12 VOY principles of true happiness
and success / by Fernando Espuelas.
p.   cm.
ISBN 1-58542-338-6
1. Self-actualization (Psychology)   I. Title.
BF637.S4E77   2004   2003070340
158.1—dc22

Printed in the United States of America
10 9 8 7 6 5 4 3 2 1

This book is printed on acid-free paper ∞

BOOK DESIGN BY LEE FUKUI

To the love of my life,
Ann Clark Espuelas

This book was directly inspired by my mentor, Jorge Etchepare. Like a father, he has guided me through challenges, opportunities, and rough paths. Muchas gracias, querido amigo. I am thankful to my mother, Martha Asenjo, who made this journey possible. The contributions of Brian Field, Ken Siman, Brian Stauffer, and John Strausbaugh are evident throughout this book. Their indefatigable dedication to this project made it a reality. I am deeply grateful.

CONTENTS

Never, never, never quit.

—Winston Churchill

LIFE IN ACTION

VOY

VOY, Spanish for "I go."

For me—and I hope soon for you, too—VOY is more than a simple word. It is a declaration of life in action.

Life is a journey. You can be a passenger, passively accepting what each day brings, or an active explorer, following your own vision and creating your own happiness and success. By living the twelve VOY principles I describe in this book, you will be on the path to self-actualization. That means you will make the distinction between your true dreams and childhood fantasies, between your true dreams and societal expectations. Then you will envision and pursue those dreams and use the powers of optimism and passionate belief in yourself to overcome whatever obstacles threaten your path. You will realize there is no predetermined future, that you create the future every day. You will achieve what you envision. You will become a happy and successful human being and an engaged member of your community.

WHAT IS SUCCESS TO YOU, and how do you reach it? Everyone's success is a deeply personal thing. Is it a new job? A new business? Maybe a better relationship with your family?

Everyone has aspirations, but there's a huge difference between those who have "a pocketful of dreams" and those who actualize their dreams and transform their lives for the better. I want to help you become one of the self-actualizers.

You can do it. You may be poor, you may not have gotten the best education, you may be stuck in a job or a life situation that you feel is holding you back. But realize now that nothing can really hold you back. Only you can prevent yourself from reaching your true goal. You may face many obstacles, but isn't that part of what it means to be alive? In a country this rich with opportunities, resources, and freedoms, there really are no excuses, only challenges. And what would life be without challenges?

We'll discuss all this in much more detail in the following chapters. But first, you must be wondering:

Who is this guy Fernando Espuelas? How would he know the challenges I'm facing?

Well, I came to this country with literally nothing. I couldn't even speak the language. My mother scrubbed toilets to barely make ends meet. But I refused, from an early age, to let any of that hold me back. I became a multimillionaire and a famous, highly successful business entrepreneur before the age of thirty-five. I started several innovative, wildly successful business ventures that changed the direction of Latin America and the world for the better. I know what it means to start with nothing but dreams, and transform those dreams into actual success.

I also know what it means to face failure, to have the bottom drop out from under you, to feel like a fool. I have firsthand experience not only in making millions of dollars, but also— and this may be even more important—in losing them. And in what it takes to pick yourself up after a loss like that, and dedicate yourself to achieving even greater success the next time out.

Let me tell you my story.

I WAS BORN IN MONTEVIDEO, Uruguay, in 1966. My early childhood was pleasant: my household pretty much upper-middle-class. My father, Carlos, was a self-made entrepreneur, having carved out a successful career in real estate. My mother, Martha, was a typical Uruguayan housewife, managing the home and raising me, an only child. I have wonderful memories of my early years with my parents. For example, most Saturday nights they would host chic cocktail and dancing parties. A few other couples would come to our house, the Tijuana Brass would play on the hi-fi, whiskeys and wine would be served with catered snacks. My parents and their friends would dance for hours.

I attended one of the most prestigious private schools in Uruguay. It was an unusually disciplined school—we had a daily report card that graded us in everything from math to standing in line in an orderly fashion. I was an above-average student, not a standout, but beginning in first grade I was enthralled by history. My uncle, Raul, an avid reader, fed my interest by reading history books with me. The hours we spent together mapping out Columbus's voyages on his atlas sealed my love of history.

But by age eight our family was in chaos. I remember my father being vicious to my mother—and my parents went through a nasty divorce. My mother wanted to get as far away from my father as possible—so far that she chose to radically change her life, and mine. She never had a nine-to-five job, and she had little education. She had few options but was driven by desperation. Some of her cousins lived in the United States, and they sent her tickets for the two of us to leave Uruguay. So she scraped together a hundred dollars, and we flew to New York.

It was 1976, and I was nine and a half years old. I spoke no English. Everything was new to me. My mother's cousins were live-in domestic workers for a wealthy woman in Greenwich, Connecticut. It was the first of many situations where we were live-in guests, not always completely welcomed, in relatives' homes. They were poor, struggling immigrants themselves in homes already crowded with extended family, the way so many Latins have lived in this country. My mother instantly set about finding work. It was a wrenching experience for her. She had left behind a comfortable household where she had domestic help and my father drove a Jaguar. She went from that to working at a garment factory all day, and then cleaned offices at night. She missed Uruguay.

I was enrolled in a number of public schools as we moved from one apartment to another. At the first school, not a soul spoke Spanish. And I spoke no English. I learned to communicate through my facility for math—my way of showing them that even though I couldn't speak English, I was not an imbecile. Luckily, at future schools there would be at least one teacher who took a special interest in me. These were teachers who helped me learn how to read and speak English rather quickly, and gave me a semblance of belonging. I still remember how excited I was when I was made a school safety guard. I got a little badge and wore it proudly.

Everything about Greenwich, Connecticut, was so different from what I was used to. In Montevideo we'd lived in a totally urban environment. Greenwich looked like the countryside to me. One cold winter day, I was walking home from school and took a left turn when I should have gone right; I got completely lost. I went up to a house and knocked on the door. I don't know how I was expecting to communicate with them, but at any rate, they just peered at me suspiciously through a side window and wouldn't open the door. I went up to the door of the next house and spoke in Spanish to the lady there. She would not let me step into her house, even though it was winter; instead, she called the police. A squad car picked me up and drove me home. Between pointing and gesturing, I got them to understand where to take me.

Eventually, my mother was able to rent a cheap apartment where she and I could live alone. The summer between fifth and sixth grades, she managed to scrape together enough money to buy our first used black-and-white TV set. That summer, I learned a lot of English by watching television—*The MacNeil-Lehrer Report* and Julia Child's *French Chef* were my favorites. I would hear the same word repeated in different contexts, on different shows, and ask, "What's that word? What's that word?" It all started to make sense to me.

By the sixth grade, I was also doing things in school that were a little . . . unusual. I was still focused on learning English, but I also started to concentrate on making money. I tried to figure out how to start a business. I got some of my friends to invest in a venture of mine; I gave them share certificates in my new company, and then used that money to set up a "bank." I think I started it with about $30. I'd lend that out to other kids, with interest. I made close to $50 that way, which was a bundle to me at the time. I also started an insurance company: We insured books, erasers, and pencils against loss.

Inevitably, my business activities at the Greenwich public school drew the attention of my teachers. They "seized the books" of my bank and insurance company and were upset that I was making all this money from other students. I explained that I was simply providing services the other kids wanted, which seemed the American Way to me. They disagreed, and shut me down.

While I was beginning to thrive in this country, my mother was finding it increasingly difficult to cope with her life in America. Everything was so different from the life she'd known. No money, nonstop work, and strained relationships with her relatives made her despondent. She would come home from work and just break down and cry.

So I was forced to become an adult at an unusually early age. With the help of Julia Child, I taught myself how to cook by the sixth grade, and dinner would be waiting for my mother when she got home. She was so pleased with my cooking skills that food became a major source of comfort to her—and me. In other words, I became fat.

Even though I was a chubby kid with a funny accent getting mocked a lot, I always had a spark, a belief that there was always something—even if I wasn't sure what it was—better awaiting me. It wasn't a belief in destiny so much as a belief that somehow I would be able to do something great. You can call it delusional, cocky—maybe just optimistic, but there it is. So what did I do with this spark of mine in the sixth grade?

Aside from going into business for myself, I decided I wanted to be president of the student government. The only problem was, there was no student government. So I created one, ran for president, and was elected. The girl who opposed me ran on a platform that was basically "Don't vote for Fernando, because he's a big, fat spic." It wasn't especially catchy, no "I like Ike" or "Click with Dick," but it still resonated with some of the other kids, who were happy to throw ethnic slurs my way.

It was an introduction to my conflicting life—here I was president but still being harassed by classmates. It was that way from the moment I arrived in Greenwich, and it made me excruciatingly aware of how different I was from my affluent Anglo classmates. Not just ethnically but economically. Everything from the clothes I wore to my mother's battered blue bomb of a Buick was so embarrassing to me I could hardly stand it. Still, I never saw myself as a "victim" or "disadvantaged." It just made me strive harder to succeed, to learn faster, to become more inventive.

At the same time that I was creating the student government, I also decided that I wanted to be the editor of the school newspaper. But here again, the school didn't have a newspaper. So I started one. I still didn't write or even speak English all that well, so I got other kids to write for it. For the time being. And in the meantime, I became an information junkie. I read *The New York Times* and every magazine I could get my hands on. And books— I devoured biographies of my heroes: Churchill, Gandhi, Alexander, Simón Bolívar, Franklin Roosevelt, Teddy Roosevelt, Isabella of Castile, Julius Caesar, and Martin Luther King, Jr.

Another way of insulating myself from the ethnic insults was to develop a great group of close friends who treated me like a "normal guy." Some of them were Anglos; but one of my closest friends was a first-generation Chinese-American. Within our group, no one cared about who was what religion, what race, any of that.

Plus, I worked. My first job was in sixth grade, pumping gas. Later, I had two paper routes. I worked in a donut shop. I was a soda jerk, making lemon-lime sodas and cherry Cokes. I dug holes for a gardener. I cut grass. I was a clerk at Woolworth's. I sold movie tickets and popcorn. When I was sixteen, I almost talked my way into the assistant manager's job at Friendly's, but the regional manager declared that I could only be the dishwasher. I cleaned out rodent and reptile cages at a pet store.

From there I was hired to do assembly work for a man who had invented a totally novel kind of computerized church organ. He paid me $125 a week, which to me was a fortune. He turned out to be a very sick individual. Five years later, when I was in college, I was having dinner at my friend's family's Chinese restaurant when a cop came in and said, "I'm looking for Fernando Espuelas." Apparently, the church organ man was a child molester, and he'd been arrested for murdering a teenager. He'd lure teenage boys with the promise of a job, then attack them. They were looking for me to testify. I think the only reason that pedophile didn't try anything with me is that I asked him for a raise, which he refused, so I quit before he could make his move.

That cop coming into the restaurant looking for me frightened me for a completely different reason. When my mother and I had sneaked out of Uruguay, we were given only short-term tourist visas. I did not have a green card until 1985, years away at that point. Once in junior high I was in our apartment on Railroad Avenue in Greenwich—which was literally next to the railroad tracks, on the third floor in a hundred-year-old railroad building. My mother was in the kitchen, and I was playing in the living room with some friends, when our dog started barking. I went to the door and found two men standing there. I sensed trouble immediately. One of them said, "We're looking for a Hispanic family." I said, "Hmm, a Hispanic family. I don't know of any around here." Between my supposedly non-Latin looks (I'm pale-skinned, tall, and have brown hair) and the decent American accent I had developed by then, I fooled them. Thank God my mother hadn't come to the door instead of me. After that scare, I became an extremely light sleeper, always wary of any sound in the night. We heard stories of immigration officers bursting into restaurant kitchens and sweeping away all the illegal immigrants working there. I felt I could be next—pulled out of a history class by dark-suited men. It was terrifying to live that way, to feel every day like a criminal.

Through my high school years, with all the pressures on both of us, my relationship with my mother began to feel the strain. Things between us became so bad that the high school administrators wanted me to try for an early college admission just to get me out of the house. She and I were finding it completely impossible to communicate.   Things got better when I went to college.

The distance helped us get perspective and appreciate each other again.

Since she first arrived in the United States, my mother had dreamed of one day returning to Uruguay and buying a house. When I had my first financial success some years later, I came back for a visit to Greenwich and took her to Manero's, a restaurant near our old apartment where we had never gone before. It was a simple Italian place—nothing fancy, but way too expensive for us when we lived in that small apartment on Railroad Avenue.

That night, we sat down and ordered our meals. Halfway through dinner, I presented her a check for $100,000 to make her dream of returning to Uruguay and buying her own place come true. She opened the envelope, saw the check, and said, "A thousand dollars! I was going to ask you for $500 to pay this month's rent!" I explained that it was one *hundred* thousand dollars and gave her a plane ticket. She responded by crying and said softly, "Fernando, I can't . . . I can't believe this." After all the pain and struggles she had been through, I was now able to provide her with a gift: the ability to return to her homeland, completely free from financial burdens.

I WAS ALWAYS determined to go to college. Given my mediocre high school grades, I concentrated on extracurricular activities. I wrote for the student newspaper and joined the debate club; my partner and I won the Connecticut state championship. Seeing my picture in the *Greenwich Times* holding up that trophy was an enormous boost to my self-confidence. I'd been mocked for my accent, so I was self-conscious about the way I spoke. Whenever I spoke one word that came out with an accent, I felt like I had failed myself. I worked on that with such intensity that today I sound like a native-born American.

So, despite my grades, all those nonacademic activities and awards were enough to get me a scholarship at Connecticut College in New London, well regarded for its liberal arts. There were few minority students—not even twenty, I believe, out of 1,600 students. I was one of maybe a half-dozen Latins in the school.

When I started college, my mother earned $7,000 a year, and a year's tuition was $11,000. The gap between my situation and my friends' was profound. I would go to a friend's multimillion-dollar house and look at the six luxury cars in the driveway. They would go on vacations in Switzerland. Their moms carried Gucci bags. And yet the way they treated me, the way so many people adopted me, is something I'm so grateful for. They knew I loved music, so they would take me to the theater and to concerts. One friend's family gave me a computer. A lot of people went out of their way to engage me. I became more confident and outgoing instead of embittered and envious.

In my freshman year I took over the campus newspaper, *The College Voice*, eventually becoming the editor in chief. I considered myself an investigative journalist-in-training and fiercely attacked the college administration in my editorials—with no reprisals. That always stayed with me. Not to sound hokey, but it was a testament to the beauty of democracy and free speech. I realized this even as a cocky, rebellious college kid. In Latin America, the authorities might have cut my throat.

My office at *The College Voice* was right next to the dance studio. That's where I first saw my future wife, Ann Clark. Ann was raised in Washington, D.C., where she'd been a child star with the Washington Ballet. I didn't get up the nerve to talk to her until we were introduced at a party. We ended up in her dorm room and talked for eight hours straight about everything from *Star Wars* to Emily Dickinson to Nixon. That was in 1987; and we've been together ever since.

I continued to work a variety of jobs all through college. My scholarship covered my tuition and board, but I still needed to earn money for my books and living expenses. One friend's father was the chief financial officer of Philip Morris, and the summer between high school and college he arranged for me to take an internship at Philip Morris's offices in New York City. I made $200 a week, a big deal. The first summer I worked in the graphics department, but for the next three I was moved into the public relations department. This job was great. I was able to see the inner workings of a large corporation—even though it was unsettling to do public relations for a giant tobacco company. Back in the late 1980s, the tobacco industry was in a state of denial about the health risks of smoking. I still have a T-shirt from that job that is cheerfully emblazoned "Smoke and Be Healthy." I was intrigued that most everybody in the public relations department embraced this slogan. They were not corporate drones or robots—they were extremely bright and creative people. I think they really believed that they were defending people's right to smoke.

After graduating from college, I decided that working in advertising would give me an opportunity to learn about a wide range of businesses. So I mailed my résumé to the top fifty advertising agencies in the country and landed interviews with five of them. The first went terribly, because I was completely clueless about what was expected of me. The agency was BBD&O, a giant among ad agencies. Two of its largest accounts were Apple and Pepsi Cola. The first thing I did when I sat down for the interview and was asked if I'd like something to drink was to ask for . . . a Coke! Then I was asked to talk about some advertisements I'd seen recently that I either liked or disliked. I decided to take the bold choice and talk about an ad I did not like. Sadly, it was an ad for Apple computers.

At this point the woman conducting the interview put down her pen, sighed, and said, "Look, let me help you out here. You know, you've got to do some preparation and reading up about

what's going on in this industry to be successful at it. You probably *will* be successful at it . . . just not here."

My next interview went much better: Wunderman Worldwide, the direct marketing division of the Young & Rubicam
agency, offered me $22,500, and I started as an assistant account
executive.

I loved my job and all the perks that came with it. I was just
out of college and had a secretary. My first clients were American
Express and General Foods. I learned how to develop a direct
marketing manual for American Express. But after about six
months there, something happened that has happened to me
many times since: I got restless and anxious. Even though I was
on the company's fast track, I wasn't ascending fast enough. So I
started to look for other job opportunities, and was soon offered
a position with Lowe & Partners, a large British agency with a
U.S. division.

But after about a year with Lowe, I started to feel unfulfilled
again. Ann and I had been talking about the possibility of living
abroad. This was in the early 1990s and Latin America was going through a monumental shift from what had been a set of
closed, crisis-driven economies to a more open, free-market system. Their own talent pool was thin and neglected, and there was
little creative or innovative thought. Argentina, for example, had
long been in a perpetual state of economic chaos. Talented people
languished or left the country, so there was a great hunger for
marketing talent—especially New York marketing talent. I took
an offer to be the managing director of Ogilvy & Mather's direct
advertising agency in Argentina. I was twenty-four and wouldn't
have this kind of opportunity in New York anytime soon. And
Argentina is close to Uruguay, where I was born.

Ann and I packed up and moved to Buenos Aires, Argentina,
in 1991. Instantly we felt astray. I didn't realize how different

Uruguay was from other Latin American countries until I went to Argentina. I thought I spoke Spanish, but when I got there I realized my Spanish had suffered terribly after living in the United States for fifteen years. This made socializing difficult. It was a lonely time for Ann and me. Worse, Argentina's society is largely closed, so the friends you make in high school end up as your friends for life. Luckily, we eventually began to meet a circle of other expatriates—mostly young people like us who'd left jobs in London and New York and all over the world to come to Argentina, where we all had positions that were far above what we would have back home. We were all navigating this new world together.

My job was to start up direct-marketing services for American Express in Argentina. I was successful and won the respect of a much-feared boss, Leandro Quilmes.

"Fernando," Mr. Quilmes said to me. "I have a great business opportunity for you. Come to the conference room at four this afternoon." What did he want with me?

The meeting was—surprisingly—filled with company bigwigs. Mr. Quilmes abruptly announced, "I just got a call from Unilever." Unilever was the agency's biggest client. "They are angry at you," he said—to all those bigwigs in the room, not to me. "They are about to take their business elsewhere. This is intolerable. I can't believe you let this happen. So I told them that, starting today, I am putting Fernando in charge of this account."

Then he turned to me and said, "And Fernando, I just want you to know that if you have to fire everyone here, go ahead and fire them. Fire all of them."

I was stunned. I think everyone in the room was.

He had given me a huge promotion, running the biggest base of business at the company. And I didn't "fire all of them," only one—the hardest decision of my young career. That aside, things went very well. The clients liked me. The agency did well that year and was hugely profitable the next—and I was responsible for much of that profit. I was elected to the board of directors when I was twenty-four.

After the lonely start, life in Argentina had become fabulous—almost. And then, as has often happened in my career, I reached the stage where I couldn't advance any farther, and by 1994 it was time to move on again. I returned with Ann to the United States—to Miami, where AT&T Latin America needed someone to run their marketing communications for them. AT&T was then one of the most prestigious companies on the planet, with about a hundred billion dollars of annual revenue, and I figured I was going to be the CEO someday. My attitude was: "I'm here, I'm going to be the CEO, now how do I get there?" I decided to prove to them that I deserved to be the CEO. I would work with absolute concentration and do so well that it would just be obvious.

So for the next nine months I worked like a maniac. Many AT&T executives were not the most ambitious workers on the planet, so I stood out quickly. I would fly to Brazil for a day, go to Argentina for a day. I made some grueling trips, then came back and worked the next day. I prided myself on that. Overnight flights into Miami from Latin America would arrive at five A.M. I'd be at my desk at eight A.M. that morning, not even tired. I was that driven.

Soon enough I was promoted, becoming the youngest managing director in the company at the age of twenty-eight. It was a milestone for me. I was there to work and create, and they gave me a $30 million budget to do just that. My rapid advancement was a source of some discomfort for the people who worked around me, many of whom were twenty-five years older than I was and had worked their way up the corporate ladder gradually.

My boss made the mistake of saying to me, "Look, you should know it took me eight years to get my last promotion." Which was the least compelling argument in AT&T's favor that I could hear. I didn't want *his* job—I wanted the CEO's job.

I got the promotion to managing director, and I suddenly felt like I'd earned a position I didn't really want. Something about the whole thing was dispiriting. So Ann and I decided to do something radical and go away for a month. I'd been working hard, and my Latin American counterparts all took month-long vacations, so why not? I went into my boss and said, "Look, I know this is weird and not done around here, but I need the time to recover."

So we went. We spent two weeks in India and two weeks in Nepal. It was the most profound experience of my life.

We started the trip in northern India, a stunningly beautiful place with ancient cities rising up out of the desert. We always stayed someplace different: from normal hotels to the maharaja's converted former palace. And then we'd walk outside and confront the crushing poverty that's everywhere in India. The contrast was haunting. We'd walk out the palace gates into this maelstrom of misery. Maybe because we were young and inexperienced in Indian society, we felt an enormous amount of guilt and sympathized with much of India's resentment toward Westerners—their sense of "Yes, we want your money, but we'd rather not have you here just the same."

Nepal was an entirely different experience. Nepal, from what we saw, was in many ways as poor as India but lacked its raw desperation, at least in terms of the urban poverty we witnessed in India. Nepal is, of course, a magnet for seekers. There is a magical quality to the country, a colorful beauty unlike that of any other place. Nepal is not just simply in the Himalayas, it is *of* the mountains, and its people believe that it is the home of the gods.

The highlight of the trip was a trek in the Annapurna range of the Himalayas. The first morning our guide, Delip, came to the Yak and Yeti Hotel, where we were staying. Delip was a friendly man who had lived for a time in the United States and spoke English well. When we stepped outside the hotel, an old school bus was waiting, with a large group of people already on board. We figured we must be hitching a ride somewhere with them. We drove out of Katmandu and started to climb up the mountains. We stopped in a couple of villages and picked up more people. Local folks. It eventually dawned on us—they were all there for us. Just Ann and me. We'd booked a trek, and this was the crew we'd be hiking with. We felt like such typical, pampered Americans: Ann and I in our Italian hiking boots, the locals in flip-flops and sandals.

We began the hike up the mountain—Ann, Delip, and I, followed by this crowd of local men lugging our tents, clothing, drinking water, and fuel for fires. Ann and I were totally unprepared for how tough this hike was going to be. We thought we'd just be taking a little walk in the hills. This is what struck us: the soaring beauty of the mountains all around us—and the fact that we felt like we were going to die of sheer exhaustion climbing them.

One of the revelations I had on that climb was that the only way to come down that mountain was to go up. That is, you actually had to travel up across a range before you could work your way back down. Metaphorically, that was a key lesson I've never forgotten. I realized that many times in life, the only solution is to push forward, regardless of the effort—you simply have to climb the next hill if you want to survive. A few months earlier there had been an accident on this mountain, when a sudden snowstorm had surprised and killed a group of hikers. They hadn't learned the lesson: They died trying to go back down the mountain the way they'd come. If they had pushed upward, they might have survived.

When we broke for lunch, it was like a scene from the height of the British Raj—all these Nepalis setting up camp and cooking lunch, with Delip bossing them around, and Ann and I collapsed on the ground, unable to lift a finger, and not having to. Meanwhile, people from nearby mountain villages, going about their grueling daily lives, passed us as they went up and down the mountain. We were especially struck by the women. The villagers were so poor they had cut down all the nearby trees for firewood, their only source of fuel. So the women had to trek some distance away for firewood. There was one woman who came down the hill with a gigantic log on her head. She couldn't have been more than five-foot-four, and she was old enough to be our mother. And there we were in our swanky Italian boots, exhausted, sprawled on the ground, moaning about our sore muscles, while she gracefully walked by with a log on her head, and our guides were scrambling to feed us lunch. And that's their life, every day, day after day after day.

I suddenly realized how ridiculously easy my life was, despite the hardships and relative poverty of my youth, despite all the hard work I'd put in and all the struggles I thought I'd been through. It struck me how absurdly easy it had been for me to be successful, compared to what billions of other people have to go through in this world.

It was a moment of enlightenment, a burst of realization. I lay there on that mountain and thought, "Oh my God, I can do anything. And I'm going to do something really, really big."

When we returned to the climb, the sheer exuberance of that thought filled me up with physical power. I began to run up the path into the mountains, just run and run and run and run—until I literally reached a fork in the road and realized that if I picked the wrong road I could disappear up there and never be seen again. So I stopped for the others to catch up.

That night, we camped on a ledge overlooking a high valley. We could see the snow-topped peaks just above us, hugging the valley on all sides. Behind us, above the ledge, was an ancient Buddhist temple where people had mediated for centuries. It had a startling presence, a beauty that defies my abilities of description.

As I stood in this palpably magical place, I thought about my life in the United States, my path so far, and what I was seeking. I had been traveling exhaustively across Latin America and had witnessed the poverty and desperation, the nepotism and corruption of the elite few who controlled all the money and all the power.

It became clear to me that night, as clear as that view of the mountains across the valley, that what had been keeping Latin Americans isolated from each other, both across social and economic castes and across national territories, had been communication barriers. If these barriers could be removed, if Latins could freely exchange ideas without intervention, without fear of political reprisals, it would be the most powerful shift in society since the arrival of the Spanish and the Portuguese in the fifteenth century. I saw the Internet as that tool that would change everything for Latins. And I felt I had this mission to be the one who brought it to them. I could see it so clearly.

For the rest of the trip I was obsessed by this vision: that this was what I was destined to do and what I was going to do. I didn't know how to do it yet—I didn't know the path, and I didn't know anything about what kind of business this was going to be. I just knew that a technology that would allow millions of people throughout Latin America to get information independently of government and media monopolies would be hugely attractive to Latins, and would change everything for them. Over a period of a few decades it could change the whole society, because it would shift the way that humans interact with each other. It would alter the power equations in societies throughout Latin America. Too often archaic governments, run by corrupt elites, imposed a self-serving will on their citizens. The Internet was a catalyst to change this reality.

I realized that the true asset of Latin America was the people. It wasn't the land, it wasn't the petroleum. It was the people, their vibrancy quelled by corrupt regimes. I realized that if you could plug the citizens of Latin America into this new technology, something revolutionary would happen.

And I went on to do that. I projected my will into the future, and I made this vision a reality.

———

I RETURNED TO AT&T a totally different person. It wasn't just that I had a mission for a specific project anymore. I had a life mission. It transcended being a managing director at AT&T, or a CEO-in-waiting. It was something much, much bigger.

It was 1995, and the Internet was still a bit into the future for many people, including my boss, who was in his mid-fifties. This was a man who hated e-mail. He would have his e-mails printed out by his secretary, then he'd handwrite answers and have his secretary type them in. He had no idea what I was talking about, but it was so obvious that I wasn't going to let this vision go that he finally said, "Okay, okay, go do this . . . 'Net' thing."

So I launched AT&T Hola in Latin America in 1996. I conceived of many of the underlying concepts of what would be called portals. I wanted to give people free e-mail accounts. (This was a year before Hotmail was launched.) AT&T vetoed that idea. We had the first search engine ever in Spanish and in Portuguese. We were the first customers on the planet for the Reuters newswire services in Portuguese and in Spanish. It was so early in the life of the Net that they actually faxed us stories. We had some of the first games on the Net, and the first online bulletin board in Latin America.

I launched the project by setting up press conferences in AT&T's five major Latin markets: Mexico, Colombia, Chile, Argentina, and Brazil. We got tremendous media coverage. We did a small promotion in Mexico City, where we put a single ad on just one radio station, saying that AT&T would be having a free Web fair where you could try out the Internet. We set up thirty or forty PCs—and something like nine thousand people showed up. They lined up for blocks. I got to see hundreds of people's first experience on the Internet. And people were enthralled. The media came in droves. It was on the front page of all the business sections. I was on television in every country.

After my success at AT&T, I decided it was time to start a new company of my own, through which I really could achieve my mountaintop vision of uniting and democratizing Latin America. And that's how StarMedia Network was born. Netscape had burst onto the scene by then, and the capital markets were suddenly interested in investigating—and investing in—this newfangled thing called the Internet. So we were riding a trend, which always makes life easier when launching a business. Latin America, meanwhile, was still on its own trend of improving and opening up its economies, and that process was becoming increasingly successful. So it seemed like the right time to do something big.

My partner, a friend since sixth grade, and I pooled our savings. We borrowed some from his family. I maxed out my credit cards and applied for new ones. At one point I was paying our rent with one credit card and using another credit card to pay off that first one, a byzantine system of financing debt with more debt.

We hired four people initially. We bought the cheapest office chairs and desks we could find. We bootstrapped and scrimped, hoping not to run out of money before this thing got off the ground. From the beginning, this was not some fun little project—this was going to be a real corporation. I kept saying, "We're not just doing a website, we're doing a media company. And one day, if we do things right, we'll be worth $100 million." I wanted everyone to understand that right from the start. I set the arbitrary date of December 15, 1996, to launch the website, which would be called StarMedia.com. To make sure it would be launched on time, I scheduled a media tour of the five countries in Latin America where I had been well received when I was at AT&T.

We confronted a high degree of uncertainty, both in terms of the business itself—nothing like this had existed before—and in terms of our ability to raise the needed capital, which, obviously, was going to be millions upon millions of dollars. We were always on the verge of running out of money. We raised a good amount by ourselves, from everyone we could think of. We were willing to talk to any potential investor. One of our four employees suggested we talk to his dentist, so I did. I did an hour-and-a-half presentation to him, and he invested $10,000. Eventually, we raised almost half a million dollars. But that wasn't nearly enough.

So we went pitching ourselves to venture capitalists, where the real millions would have to come from. And that was hard going. We made presentations in New York, some in Miami, many in Silicon Valley. We had more than fifty meetings, and received an overwhelming, unanimous response: "No." Sometimes their objections were good ones; for instance, they doubted that the local telephone companies and infrastructure in Latin America would be dependable enough for a venture like this. That was certainly a reasonable concern. And sometimes their objections were simply ridiculous and racist—like that of a top venture capitalist in New York, who told me my presentation was persuasive and passionate, "but you know, Latin America is just that blob south of Texas." We moved forward.

We launched StarMedia.com at the end of 1996, but by early '97 we had little capital left. StarMedia.com was great, as far as it went. It had e-mail, chat rooms, bulletin boards, personal ads, classifieds, interactive stories. I was proud of the site, but it was a small step toward our ultimate vision.

Here is that vision: What we launched as StarMedia.com focused on community services. The e-mail, the chat rooms, the bulletin boards, and so forth were designed as early mechanisms to aggregate people into what were virtual communities. We said from the beginning that StarMedia.com was not an Internet portal but a far grander concept, one that didn't even exist at that point. Today everyone understands what you mean by "virtual community," but in 1996 and 1997 it was still a novel idea. We reached back into history and revived a very old idea of civilization, which is to create a space where people can gather and exchange information. The Greeks called it the agora. For the Romans, it was the forum. This concept has been central to all Latin civilization ever since. In cities, there's the plaza, the one central square where everyone gathers to exchange information.

What we created on the Internet was a virtual central square, where users could gather to meet, get information, pay their bills, get the news, and purchase other goods and services. And we were creating that central square not just for one city in Latin America, not just for one country, but for all the Latin world.

This was a radical message to announce in Latin America, where insular nationalism was pivotal to citizen identity. Latins have been raised to believe that the people on the other side of the mountain are monsters, not to be trusted, and not particularly smart. Which is, obviously, the kind of mind-set that countries use to justify themselves as political units, and to justify maintaining their often quite arbitrary national borders. It's the old strategy of a government convincing its people to define themselves as being against some *other* people, thereby creating a skewed sense of group identity that overcomes all the internal differences (such as ethnic, racial, and class differences) that exist within almost all Latin countries.

So for us to come out and declare that we were going to erase those borders and create an opportunity for the next generation of Latin America to reunify the continent with this technology—that was radical (the media called me "the new Simón Bolívar"). We wanted to redefine history—and I think that, in fact, is what has happened. We're still in the early stages of it, but the reality is that through these interactive services, Colombians are meeting Mexicans, and Venezuelans are meeting Chileans, and that simply couldn't happen before. People are discovering each other, and thereby changing the course of history, as they increasingly define themselves as Latins as well as Mexicans, Chileans, Argentines. They have an actual relationship with someone on the other side of the mountain. I now believe that the youth of Latin America, being so disproportionately large a segment of the population (a majority of the population is under age twenty), will grow up with a completely different consciousness of what it is to be Latin and what Latin America means: that we are diverse but bound by a common culture, common histories, common experiences that define us as a people. And with Latin American governments becoming increasingly open to cooperating with each other economically, we're going to see a real coming together across borders and across generations. StarMedia's vision of pan–Latin Americanism was a historical turning point for Latins around the world.

That was my goal, and my motivation. It was social. It was political. I think I got so much media coverage in Latin America because I was speaking in this new and different way. Of course, I got a lot of attention for the business angle, for taking this little start-up public and quickly growing it into a $4 billion company. But the big picture was always what I was presenting, which was revolutionary and, to some, a pipe dream. One Latin business journalist called me Don Quixote. She treated me like some sort of idiot savant—as in "Oh, it's so sweet that you want to unify Latin America, but don't you understand we all hate each other? And that the politicians won't allow it?"

That is, unfortunately, how people in Latin America have thought for centuries, and StarMedia went about squelching that mind-set.

We broke down other false barriers as well. We operated on a gender-blind hiring policy. There was no sort of barrier in Star-Media if you were a woman. In fact, the way it worked out, most of our executives were women. This may not sound like such a huge thing, but in male-dominated Latin America? It was not only new, people thought it was crazy. But this was another message we were sending: We're a young company, and we're not going to be held back by an antiquated tradition that ignores half of the population.

That was the vision, anyway. But by the spring of '97 we thought we were going to have to close shop and call it a day— nice try, but no go. Then Chase Manhattan Bank invested $2 million in us, which immediately made us a credible player. Over the next four months, we raised another $12 million. Six months later, we did the single biggest private placement for an Internet company to date—$80 million. And now we were a big company to watch in the Internet sector. Six months later, we did the first IPO for a Latin technology company. The first day, the stock closed at a level that gave the company a valuation of $1.6 billion.

From maxed-out credit cards to over $1.5 billion. Not bad for a kid from Uruguay who'd come to this country with nothing.

By any measure, StarMedia was a spectacular success. Star-Media had 25 million unique users a month, which made us the seventh-largest website in the world and the only non-English-language supersite in the world. We had five hundred global advertisers. It was much more than just a website. We offered a series of products online, with several different portals. You could get information via broadband or cell phone. We were an integrated new media company.

We acquired eleven other companies. We eventually raised $500 million of capital. We maxed out our staff at around twelve hundred people. We opened up local operations in eleven countries. At our headquarters in New York alone, we had four hundred employees.

Yes, StarMedia was a giant among Internet media companies. I was a wealthy man and a global media celebrity. *Time* magazine honored me as one of the "Leaders for the New Millennium." The World Economic Forum included me among its elite "Global Leaders of Tomorrow." I received *Latin Trade* magazine's prestigious Bravo Award. I won the *New York* Magazine Award. I met with the presidents of the United States and several Latin American nations, the secretary-general of the United Nations, and senators, congressmen, and ambassadors.

And then I lost it all.

ON AUGUST 6, 2001, three days before my thirty-fifth birthday, I was in my corner office at StarMedia headquarters in lower Manhattan. My board of directors was in the next room. I had scheduled what we called an "all hands" meeting. That meant that everyone in the company was present—not just everyone in the New York office but everyone in all our other offices throughout Latin America, hooked in via telephone and webcast. We called it "all hands" as in "all hands on deck." The company was a ship, and I was the captain.

And the ship was taking water from all sides. Like all the

other ships on the Internet ocean, we had been struck by a tidal wave: the abrupt, near-complete collapse of the Internet economy that began in the spring of 2000.

But for us, it wasn't just a tidal wave; it was a tidal wave, followed by a tsunami, simultaneously hitting with an underwater vortex and a hurricane, while the ship was engulfed by a gargantuan octopus. The collapse of the Internet marketplace coincided with a sudden and unexpected collapse of the Latin American economy, which coincided with the bottom dropping out of the media marketplace, which helped drive a stampede in the stock market, which was just one of the catalysts that caused the capital markets to shut down, which coincided with the onset of a general recession in the U.S. economy. Any one of these events would have presented certain challenges, but all of these factors coming together at the same time created a catastrophic situation for us. The bursting of the Internet bubble had been roughly simultaneous with an economic meltdown in Argentina, causing ripple effects throughout Latin America. The Brazilian and Mexican economies slowed down, the U.S. economy was grinding down, and it became impossible to raise new money. Our ability to buy other businesses withered because our stock declined. All of the companies around us, whether advertisers or potential partners, were facing the same stress, which meant they could no longer buy services from us. Our stock, like that of virtually every other Internet company, tumbled.

I had to take responsibility for our desperate situation and find a way forward. I was optimistic that my plan would right the ship and position the company for future growth. But the board of directors and I violently disagreed on the solution. I therefore had two choices: I could stay, and provoke a nasty public war with the board, or I could resign and hand over the helm to someone new, in the hope that I could spare the company this ugly conflict. I decided to leave. In retrospect, that is my only regret. To this day, I know in my brain and heart that I had the means to make StarMedia a long-term winner in the Internet industry.

I announced my decision to leave the company in an extremely emotional meeting. Connected through a webcast to eleven countries, I told the people who built StarMedia that I was leaving. An AP article reported how staff wept and gave me a five-minute standing ovation at the end of my resignation speech. In that speech—which I paused at one point, because I started to cry myself—I spoke about how proud I was of what we'd been able to achieve in our great adventure together, and how we'd changed the lives of millions of people.

Maybe you can imagine what a devastating feeling that was for me. Maybe in your own life you've thought that you had achieved your life's goal, made your "dream come true"—and then lost it.

But with the anguish, I also felt an enormous sense of *release*. I had been struggling mightily to keep the company afloat in high seas for a year by then. If I'm responsible for something, I'm responsible for it twenty-four hours a day. For five years, StarMedia had been all I thought about, all I talked about.

I look at all of that with no rancor, with far more pride than pain. I came out of it with my optimism intact. Tired, but whole. The tactical defeat was accompanied by a new freedom, a new opportunity to go out and achieve something even greater.

Does that sound insanely optimistic? I admit, many people would have just curled up on the floor in a fetal position at that point and given up. Believe me, I felt the urge. I was sad, I was exhausted, and I was worse than broke—the steep drop in StarMedia's stock value had taken virtually all of my personal wealth with it, and I was facing some enormous debts. Because I believed in our company and our mission, I had never sold a

single StarMedia share or stock option. I personally lost close to
$500 million.

By all logical analysis, I should have gone into bankruptcy
and hidden out in the back of a pickup truck somewhere. Instead,
I rented a little cabin in the Vermont woods and spent a week just
hiking, sometimes fifteen miles a day, and coming back to cook
myself incredibly large, Uruguayan-style barbecues. Ann stayed
in New York; she knew I needed the time alone to relax and sort
things out in my mind. She was faultlessly supportive and understanding of the stress I had gone through. After all, she had shared
it—the highs and the surprising stress of success, the lows and the
painful stress of defeat. Our marriage was stronger than ever.

And, just as I'd come down from that mountaintop in Nepal
with a new mission, I came out of those Vermont woods with
a new mission. I was going to come back, and I was going to
come back even bigger than before. Betting against me is always
a bad choice. I came back from that week in Vermont, got on
the telephone, and started sharing my vision for my next project: VOY.

Just as StarMedia.com was much more than a website, VOY
is far more than a media company. VOY's goal is to give Latins
in the United States and Latin America a full range of services and
tools they can use to achieve self-actualization. Those tools include information, education, and financial services. In addition
to books like this one, VOY is reaching out with its message
through television programs, the Internet, and newspapers. VOY
will partner with established vocational and distance-learning
schools to provide skills to people seeking to better themselves,
find more gainful employment, and move up in the world. We will
establish ongoing seminars in leadership where individuals will
be inspired by some of today's leading thinkers. VOY will also
collaborate with financial institutions in creating services that are

targeted to the needs of Latins in this country, including personal credit, small-business loans, and other tools allowing personal financial freedom. In providing all these services and creating new opportunities, VOY will have a major impact in shaping and strengthening the future of Latins in the United States and Latin America.

I have spent much of the last three years traveling the country, speaking with students, families, and community and business leaders. Again and again, I hear that people are worried, fearful, lost. This book is the first step in bringing the transformative power of VOY to a large audience. We will spread a message of hope, of demonstrating a path to personal fulfillment. Just as the power of communication was visionary to Latins in the 1990s, today the message of self-actualization, of finding your own success, of creating your own happiness, is just as powerful.

As I was envisioning VOY, my friend Roberto Hernandez provided inspiration essential to my comeback. Roberto is a self-made billionaire in Mexico. He sold his bank, Banamex, the largest bank in Mexico, to CitiGroup for $12 billion. Like me, he had started with nothing. He used to take fruit from his father's orchard outside of Mexico City, drive it into the city in a truck, and sell it in the street.

Roberto invited Ann and me to his ranch. He has astounding properties in Mexico, and the most beautiful esthetic in terms of land; he once bought a mountain that could be seen from his land and turned it into a national park so that no one could build on it. We met when StarMedia tried to secure a deal with Banamex. It didn't go through, but he and I struck up a friendship.

We were sipping tequila before dinner at his ranch, and I said, "Roberto, I feel like a schmuck," and complained about how much I had lost.

He replied, "Fernando, I wouldn't worry a second about that.

In 1968, when I was your age, I had a very sizable fortune. Then I made a huge bet on the silver market and I lost everything. And here I am today. I have no doubt that you're going to build it all again, only much bigger and better this time."

Many people have said things like that to me, but it meant so much coming from this man. He had lived it. It wasn't theoretical; he had lost a huge fortune.

It is very clear to me, as clear as when I saw the Internet from that mountaintop in Nepal, that I have a duty, a responsibility, a mission—to be a leader. And with that in mind, I got to work on building the media company I knew VOY had to be—a company that would enable people to achieve their own dreams.

————

WHICH LEADS US to the book you hold in your hands. You *can* achieve your dreams, and I want to help you do that. I'm offering you the benefit of what I have learned and how I have achieved the things I have.

In the following chapters, I'm going to explain twelve principles of true happiness and success that I have developed from my own experiences and from studying extraordinary people. There are also exercises that will help you focus, plan, and achieve a life in action.

VOY, I go.

Come, take this journey with me.

Define Success and Happiness

*Twenty years from now you will be more
disappointed by the things you didn't do than by
the ones you did do. So throw off the bowlines.
Sail away from the safe harbor. Catch the trade
winds in your sails. Explore. Dream. Discover.*

— MARK TWAIN

What is success? There is no one answer.
Success is an extremely personal affair. There are as many kinds
of success as there are people in the world.

At its most general, **success is being able to look back and realize that for each stage of your life, you were able to achieve the
most that you could.** It means being able to look back without re-
grets—not because you achieved great wealth or fame but because you were able to fulfill yourself as a human being.

We are at a critical juncture in our lives. The world has
changed dramatically in the last few years. We entered not only a
new millennium in 2000 but an era of insecurity and doubt, of
hostility and fear. Today, optimistic plans for personal growth and
fulfillment seem to be in constant jeopardy. Those people lucky
enough not to have lost their jobs, their fortunes, or their savings

cling to what little they have. Instead of hope for the future, people now pray to avoid ruin. People who still have jobs forego all hope of advancement or career shifts, while young people confront the bleakest job market in decades.

In this troubled and daunting new world, people are searching for meaningful ways to shift their lives, to fortify themselves from the inside and find a way to unlock long-buried dreams. The traditional definition of success, long tied to making money, is not satisfying anymore. People increasingly—and correctly—identify success with fulfillment. The need for a message of hope, a message demonstrating that a path to personal fulfillment can still be mapped during these chaotic times, is critical.

You must know this feeling yourself, or you wouldn't be holding this book in your hands. I want to give you the inspiration to aid you in your quest for true happiness and personal success.

In my own life, as you've just read, I've gone through many stages of confusion, poverty, and pain—but I never lost my inner direction, my drive, my sense that I could achieve great things if I tried. Every day when I get up I realize that I have a responsibility to myself, my family, and to the rest of society to do the very best I can that day. That has been my life philosophy since I was a boy.

You have a responsibility to yourself to be the most happy, the most successful, the most actualized person you can be, too. It's your responsibility to find the tools and the road maps to that personal success. You can do it. And the change you will go through when you make that transformation to a fully self-actualized human being will astound you.

Success doesn't just happen to people. Success is not winning the lottery. Statistically, you're more likely to have a jet engine drop on your head than to win millions of dollars in the lottery. So while you're not likely to be "lucky" enough to win the lottery, you can make your own luck. Luck is what you create for yourself in your daily life. It's the people you surround yourself with and how you react to them. It's the opportunities for which you make yourself available. It's a process of being ready for success. It's an attitude. If you expect to win, and you create circumstances where you do win, this process develops in you a sense of optimism, a positive energy and momentum, that can be very powerful.

I'm not one of those self-help gurus who's going to tell you he has come up with a foolproof formula for success. Anyone who tells you that is most likely a con artist. The only successful person who's going to come out of one of those expensive seminars is probably the guy giving it—he's successfully conned you out of your money. There is no universal formula for success. But we can observe success in action, and learn from it, and apply certain principles to our own lives.

MONEY WILL NOT BUY YOU HAPPINESS

Let's begin with what success and happiness are not:

Success is *not* money.

Money will not buy you happiness.

I know you've heard that many times before: "Money can't buy me love," and so on.

But I'm here to tell you it's one of those clichés that is absolutely true: Money cannot buy happiness. There seems to be no direct correlation between money and happiness. I know that from my personal life. Having millions did not in itself make me a happier person. What made me happy was the act of creating a company and the services that resulted in all that money—not the money itself. I had a dream and went out and made it a reality. What made me a success was creating a way to connect Latin

If you follow your bliss, you will always have your bliss, money or not. If you follow money, you may lose it, and you will have nothing.

—JOSEPH CAMPBELL

people to each other and give them a powerful new voice they never had before. Making money while doing that was purely incidental.

I know this is true for others as well. I know many people who are "successful" by traditional money measures: They're wealthy, and they have power, status, beautiful homes, great cars. And some of them are the most unhappy—and by my definition least successful—people I have ever met.

The New York Times recently ran an in-depth profile of a sixty-seven-year-old man struggling to survive on $1,100 a month from Social Security, supplemented with what he could make cleaning toilets and making deliveries. The shocking thing was that this man had once been an extremely successful and powerful mover and shaker on Wall Street—one of the "Masters of the Universe," as they're called. His personal fortune reached $20 million at one point. He had a chauffeur for his $100,000 Mercedes and thought nothing of spending $40,000 to fly all his friends to his vacation home for a weekend party.

And yet for all his power, status, and luxurious lifestyle, this was a deeply unhappy and frustrated man. He drank heavily. He was combative with his bosses, who he felt didn't properly appreciate him, and bounced from firm to firm. He was twice divorced.

And at the age of fifty-seven he became addicted to crack cocaine. This was an Ivy League–educated Wall Street heavyweight, yet he was "hitting the pipe," as he recalled, forty to fifty times a day. The addiction ruined him. He lost everything. He was evicted from his luxurious penthouse and was homeless for a while. The downward spiral continued for several years. When interviewed by the *Times*, he was clean and sober, but his career and reputation were in shambles.

The article ended with an observation by his daughter.

"Money isn't that important," she said. *"It certainly didn't make my father happy."*

On a much lighter note, there's Dick McDonald, one of the brothers who owned the original little McDonald's hamburger stand. He was often asked if he was sorry that they sold the idea and the McDonald's name to entrepreneur Ray Kroc. Kroc paid the two brothers about enough for each of them to buy a new Cadillac, then went on to create a global empire using their name and their idea.

Dick McDonald always said he didn't regret selling out to Kroc in the least. He knew that if he had gone along with Kroc as he built the McDonald's empire, he would have ended up in a corporate office tower somewhere, surrounded by assistants and tax accountants and lawyers, worrying about the business and his money all the time. It was not a life Dick McDonald desired. Even though he would have been a billionaire, he knew in his heart that it wouldn't have made him *happy.*

I'm not asking you to feel sorry for billionaires. But you don't have to be a wealthy person to know the truth of what I'm saying. You can think of examples from your own life when you saved up and finally were able to buy something you thought you really wanted, something you thought was really going to change your life. A big stereo, a new car, a designer dress. Be honest: Once you got that new thing, did it really make you a happier person? Did that new stereo make you feel more fulfilled as a human being? Now that you have that big stereo, you find yourself always having to buy new CDs to feed it. You still have to drive that brand-new car to your same old job every day, so that you can make your monthly car payments. You may enjoy having those new things, but can you honestly say your life has been changed by them?

Michael Lewis's book *Liar's Poker* is an insightful insider's view of Wall Street, a culture that does equate happiness and success solely with money. As a college graduate in the mid-1980s, Lewis entered the training program at the then-giant bond-trading firm of Salomon Brothers. He wasn't there because he had any real interest in the bond market as a career; in fact, like most of his fellow trainees, he knew absolutely nothing about Salomon Brothers except that it was a place where he might make an enormous amount of money very quickly. Lewis depicts the entire firm, from trainees to the highest executives, as motivated solely by making money—not doing anything useful or even fun with it, just making it, for themselves and for the firm. The latter was not out of any pride in or loyalty to the firm, but only because it gave an individual more power in the firm's vicious pecking order.

Lewis describes a corporate culture of sheer vulgarity and meanness, an uncivilized jungle where the only human emotions are the cruelty of the bosses and the fearful degradation of their groveling subordinates. Even the bosses, though they're multi-millionaires, seem miserable. Their personal fortunes bring them no joy, no satisfaction, no peace of mind; even with their millions, they are as unhappy, as overstressed, as insecure as the lowest trainee. They eat and drink like cartoon gluttons, but they take no enjoyment from it; food is just fuel to power them through their extremely stressful business day, which they spend screaming at one another and their clients. They have trophy wives and expensive homes and cars, but they take no real joy there, either—they're all just status symbols that they flaunt at each other, more like male chimps than human beings.

Lewis may have been exaggerating to make a point, but I know from firsthand observation that the heart of his depiction is true. I'm an entrepreneur, so when I speak on college campuses a fair percentage of the students in the audience are business majors going for their MBAs. They come to see me because I've made money and they want to make a lot of money, too. I am a symbol of what they want to be.

When I ask them *why* they want to go into the business world, why they want to be entrepreneurs, their answers can be heartbreaking. Because so often they sound like the young trainees in Lewis's book: They're just doing it because they've been told that's where they'll make the most money. This society has trained them to believe that making money is an absolute goal in itself. They believe that making a lot of money will somehow make them happy, even if it means suffering the soul-deadening horrors of working in a corporate jungle like the one described in *Liar's Poker.*

I'm probably a bit of a puzzle and a disappointment to some of these students, since I don't give them handy pointers for going out into the corporate world and making a zillion dollars just to make a zillion dollars. I tell them that being an entrepreneur happens to be my way of being creative in the world, of producing something that didn't exist before. I haven't done any of it for the money, even though I have made a lot of money doing it. I did it because envisioning business ventures that have a real impact in society, and then being able to make that dream a reality, is what drives me. It's my passion; it's my creative expression, my version of writing a symphony or climbing Mt. Everest. I am convinced that the passion I feel for what I do and the excitement I derive from it every day comes directly from my having chosen the work that is going to make me truly happy.

Sadly, many young people just starting out in the world don't even believe they can make such a choice. They live in a society where all too often independent thinking is discouraged. Many of those students were raised to believe that the most they can expect out of their working lives is to go to college and get their

MBAs and become anonymous lifelong worker bees in a giant corporate hive. A lot of those young people are going to wake up one day at their desks and realize that they've been leading completely unfulfilling lives. They may be making good money, they may have healthy 401(k) accounts and be able to take regular ski vacations, but they're miserable.

I'm not saying that everyone in the corporate world is unhappy. But many are. They're not unhappy because a corporate career is an intrinsically bad thing, but because it's wrong *for them*. It's got nothing to do with their actual talents and their true desires. They're not creating anything. They're not fulfilling themselves in those jobs. They're just paying the bills.

That condition, obviously, extends far beyond the corporate office. We all know people who feel trapped in their jobs, in all walks of life. They know somehow that it's not where they ought to be, not the way they should really be using their time and talents.

The most important lesson I've learned so far in life about what happiness means to me did not come when I made $500 million, but when I lost it. The old saying "That which does not kill you makes you stronger" really is true. Challenges and setbacks *do* make you stronger, force you to grow. When I lost all that money, it forced me to face and analyze what it is that drives me as a human being, what truly makes me happy and unhappy. I realized that what makes me happy is being creative and having a real impact in the world—not just having money.

When I said this in a speech to Columbia University students, one of them countered, "Well, but money's not *not* important. You need money to do what you want to do."

And that's true. It's a balanced, nuanced equation. In this culture, however, you're taught that money is *the* path to happiness: Win the lottery and all your dreams will come true. It's much more useful and realistic to think of money as a bridge or a tool by which you get to do the things you want to do. But to focus on money as the key ingredient in the formula is the route to failure.

YOU CAN'T CONSUME HAPPINESS

The surgeon general has declared obesity the fastest-growing cause of disease and death in America. Weight-related health problems have reached epidemic levels. More than half of all Americans are overweight or obese. The number of overweight children in America doubled between 1986 and 1998. The rate of increase was even higher for African-American and Latin kids. An estimated twelve hundred people die every day from weight-related illnesses, including diabetes, various types of cancer, coronary artery disease, and hypertension. Hundreds of thousands of overweight children in this country are at increased risk of severe weight-related problems such as kidney failure and stroke.

It is not the man who has little, but the man who craves more, who is poor.

—SENECA

Why are Americans getting so fat? Some people say America is such a rich country, where food is so abundant and affordable for the vast majority of people, that it's only natural we're always stuffing our faces. But Europe and Canada are also wealthy societies where food is readily available, and they don't experience anything remotely like America's obesity problem. Evidently, the easy availability of food is not the real issue.

People also blame the types of food Americans consume—fast food, snacks, and soft drinks. It's true that Americans eat far too much of those high-fat, high-sugar, low-nutrition types of food. Improved dietary habits would directly result in better health.

But there's a good reason why not a single lawsuit blaming Oreos or Big Macs for Americans' weight problems has even made it to trial. Instinctively, I think we all know that junk food isn't the problem, but merely the *symptom*. I think we all realize that Americans are trying to satisfy some sort of deep need through overeating. That they're trying to quiet a gnawing hunger that's spiritual and emotional, not really physical.

Why? What is that hunger Americans can't seem to satisfy?

My theory is that this culture has been traumatized by the constant bombardment of consumerism that equates money with success and consumption with happiness. We are pounded into submission by a nonstop barrage of commercials and advertisements urging us to buy a bigger car, own a new home, go on a more expensive vacation, get a whole new wardrobe—and, yes, drink another soda and eat another fatty cheeseburger. We are told every day in a thousand ways that we will not, cannot be happy unless we acquire and consume these things. Our self-esteem is under constant attack from the suggestion that we aren't good enough until we can have that fancier car or bigger house. But of course, since the economy is founded on a continual cycle of consumption, we're also told that we'll *never* acquire enough, *never* consume enough to be truly happy and successful. We must always eat more, buy more, acquire more.

No wonder we eat until our arteries clog and our hearts explode. We're trying to satisfy a hunger that can never be quieted.

Remember in the introduction, where I described my own problem with overeating as a kid? I didn't become fat because I had a real physical hunger. Eating all the time was my one way of feeding my insecurities, my worries, my fears. If you see me today, you'd never know I was a fat kid. I learned to seek happiness in less self-destructive ways.

It's not only through overeating that we exhibit this deeper, unquenchable hunger. We are urged to "overeat" in all sectors of our lives. We are taught that we will never have enough money, or enough power, or enough cars, or a big enough house to be truly happy.

In a very real sense, that's true. None of that *will* ever make you happy, no matter how much of it you accumulate or devour. But you're not supposed to know that. You're supposed to keep eating.

We're all driven by this false need to consume. It affects the very rich in this country as severely as it does the poor and striving. Even billionaires in this society somehow can't seem to earn enough or own enough to feel satisfied.

There's the well-known case of a certain billionaire who since the 1990s has been building the largest private mansion in the Hamptons, the resort area on the tip of Long Island frequented by the rich and famous. The estate this man is creating is so vast, one newspaper article reported that it needs to be seen from the air for its size to be truly grasped. When completed it will dwarf the already opulent mansions of his millionaire neighbors. The large scale of the ongoing construction project has disrupted the lives of those neighbors and made him a *persona non grata* in the area. There are even concerns about the environmental impact of such a gargantuan building project.

This is a man, by the way, who has attained his vast wealth through junk bonds, through exploiting distressed companies for his personal gain, and through owning mining companies that have been charged with illegal dumping and polluting practices in both North and South America.

Clearly, this man is trying to feed a hunger that can never be satisfied. If he weren't building a hundred-thousand-square-foot palace, he might well weigh three hundred pounds. The billionaire's gluttony has just found a different outlet than the overeater's. Whether it's $9.99 all-you-can-eat dinners or $100 million mansions, they're both trying to feed an insatiable emotional need.

And neither the billionaire builder nor the obese glutton will ever satisfy that hunger. The billionaire can go on consuming businesses until he owns the world. The glutton can eat every burger and french fry McDonald's can produce. Neither of them will achieve happiness that way.

You cannot consume happiness from outside. Happiness has to come from inside. Happiness is not passive. It is active. It is not a material object you can acquire or eat or own. It is a state of being you create.

Do Not Put Off Happiness — Seek It Now

When you arise in the morning, think of what a precious privilege it is to be alive—to breathe, to think, to enjoy, to love.

— Marcus Aurelius

In American society, a combination of the Puritan tradition, the Protestant work ethic, and the Roman Catholic belief that "suffering is good for the soul" dovetails nicely with what is expected of us in the working world. As a result, we're trained to put off happiness until some distant future. In the religious sphere, we don't expect to be happy until we die and go to heaven—*if* we've been good enough and suffered enough in life.

The working world's equivalent of heaven is, of course, retirement. In both cases, we're offered deferred happiness, a *potential* for happiness in the future. In return, we resign ourselves to suffering and toiling away in our daily, workaday lives. We accept our lot in life, however unsatisfying that is now, with the hope and expectation that we'll be happy . . . someday.

Along the way, we're offered some temporary rewards to keep us from becoming entirely miserable with our lives: money, power, status, consumer goods. But nothing about this system encourages us to seek our true happiness in the here and now. In fact, these temporary rewards, and the promise of a deferred happiness, actually work to distract us from seeking the true happiness that comes from self-actualization.

I would not presume to question anyone's religious beliefs or their ideas of heaven. But I am highly skeptical of a system that encourages us to slave away our entire adult lives at what may be empty, unrewarding jobs just to be allowed to retire at the age of sixty-five. Retirement strikes me as a very paltry reward for decades of faithful drudgery in the workplace.

Retirement can even be deadly. Among males, especially, there's the phenomenon "death by retirement." A man has spent his entire adult life working, "being productive," perhaps being important and powerful and responsible. In retirement, he suddenly finds himself with literally no occupation for his time; in others' eyes he's no longer important, not powerful anymore, responsible only for his free time. He suddenly has nothing to do and all the time in the world in which to do it. Retired Americans are encouraged to spend all their time engaged in the sort of pleasant but meaningless "leisure activities" the rest of us limit to weekends and vacations. They go fishing, play golf, travel, shop, go out to dinner or a movie.

Most of us look forward to such a lazy, carefree existence in our golden years. But beware of what you wish for. It's the abrupt switch from an active work life to this passive life of limitless leisure that quite literally kills some retirees in the first few years. They simply cannot manage the adjustment. Depression and boredom are bad for your health.

Not all retirees succumb to the allures of endless indolence. Many people lead active, engaged lives after retiring. They start second careers, do volunteer work, explore talents or skills they never had time to develop before. But here again, I am forced to wonder: Did they really have to wait until they were sixty-five to take up watercolors or volunteer at the tutoring center for disadvantaged children? If that's what they really wanted to do with their lives, why did they have to wait until their lives were three-fourths over?

When I was at AT&T, many of my colleagues were literally only working for the day when they could retire. The attitude was

"Sure, my job is stressful and unfulfilling, my career as an anonymous cog in this corporate machine is ultimately without meaning, but I'll put in my years and eventually I'll retire and won't that be sweet."

Well, maybe it is, maybe it isn't. Maybe you'll reach retirement age, maybe the job stress will kill you with a heart attack before you get there. Or maybe you'll retire and find that having nothing to do for the rest of your life isn't all it's cracked up to be. The shock might kill you before you even get to enjoy any of that boundless free time.

Take the case of a hero of mine, Roberto Goizueta. He was a Cuban immigrant who worked his way up the corporate ladder to become the CEO of Coca-Cola. I admired him tremendously when I was growing up. He was a Latin figure with enormous power in this country when there were very, very few. He worked hard all his life, was a celebrated success, had earned and saved a lot of money, and was planning for his retirement—and he died at sixty-five, before he got the chance to enjoy any of it. What a tragedy. In his case it was not "death by retirement." He'd been a heavy smoker all his life and died of cancer.

Then, too, as they say, "You might get hit by a bus." People are usually joking when they say it, but it's no joke to me. Two of my grandparents were killed in auto accidents. That's always been a powerful lesson for me, knowing that any day I could be looking left when a bus or a car comes at me from the right. No matter how well I've planned for the future, I can't prevent something like that from happening. The terrible events of September 11, 2001, made this lesson brutally clear to all of us.

That's why I say **don't put off your quest for happiness to some distant, theoretical future.** Begin your journey now.

HAPPINESS RESULTS FROM SELF-ACTUALIZATION

By self-actualization, I mean a state where you're realizing your highest potential.

I've met many people who aren't rich or famous but are tremendously successful, and they're happy. They've found themselves through teaching, or being an artist, or being a lawyer, or through running a small but satisfying business.

Success is finding that vocation in your life that allows you to be the very finest person you can be. And that's a very personal affair. Success is different for each of us. And each of us has to take our own path to achieve it. That path may *involve* money, but it has nothing to do with *making* money.

There's a luxury hotel in Manhattan where one of the bartenders has been working for more than thirty years. Every year he's rated by *New York* magazine as "the best bartender in New York." It's fun to watch this man do his job. He's in his element. He's putting on a show. He serves the right drinks at the right time with the right comment. He draws on his decades of experience and history at the hotel, and can tell you wonderful anecdotes about the famous people who've come into his bar over the years. You realize as you watch him that this man is *happy*. This obviously doesn't have much to do with money—he makes what a bartender makes. It has to do with working in an environment in which he can be creative.

I met a woman recently who'd been a public school teacher for years, and finally became so frustrated with the bureaucracy and the failures built into the school system that she decided to start her own school. She went out into the community and raised enough money to start a middle school. Now she identifies poor, inner-city students who have fallen years behind in their learning, and takes them out of the usual public school situation that was

Happiness: The full use of your powers along lines of excellence.

—JOHN F. KENNEDY

hopelessly failing to educate them. By the time they've completed her school, they've raised their skills up to the grade level where they should be. This woman is obviously a spectacular success. She's taking hundreds of kids a year and transforming their lives for the better, and by extension transforming our society. And again, her success has nothing at all to do with her personal financial gain.

Dan Klores is a highly successful public-relations man in New York City. Michael Jackson, Jennifer Lopez, Jay Leno, and P. Diddy are a few of his clients. He hobnobs with the rich and famous. His services are in constant demand.

But in his heart Klores always knew public relations wasn't his true calling. "It was never satisfying, no matter how much money and so-called 'influence' I had," he told *The New York Times*. "In a sense, I've been in an emotional prison for twenty years, trapped."

What he wanted to do was make documentary films. "I have things to say, to express, and they are, I hope, worthwhile." In his early fifties, he took time off from his firm, invested his own money, and made his first film, a modest, touchingly personal account of his boyhood friends growing up in Brooklyn, *The Boys of Second Street Park*. He created something close to his heart, actualized a lifelong dream, and it clearly meant far more to him—and to others—than all the millions he'd made designing press junkets for movie stars. As I write this, *The Boys* is in theaters, and he's begun work on a second film.

Think of people you know in your own life who are not rich, are not famous, may be doing something that our society in general would not consider "glamorous" or "prestigious"—and yet they're happy. They're doing what they need to do to be fulfilled as a human being. That's a successful person.

The term *self-actualization* was coined by a psychologist,

Abraham Maslow. Maslow described a "hierarchy of needs," which can be imagined as a pyramid with five levels. At the bottom of the pyramid are our most basic physiological survival needs: things like air, food, and water.

These most basic needs must be satisfied, Maslow believed, before we turn our attention to higher levels of needs. These levels, as we climb the pyramid, are safety and shelter, then love and belonging, then the esteem of our fellows, and at the top, the need for self-actualization. Maslow called the lower four levels deficit needs, or D-needs. He meant that if you don't have something from one of these levels—if you have a deficit of water, for example—the need to find it takes precedence over everything else. If you're dying of thirst, it's more important to you than food, or sex, or shelter, and certainly more than love or esteem. If, on the other hand, you have plenty of water—if you can just walk to the sink and pour a glass whenever you want—it ceases to become a need at all. You simply don't think about it. Then you turn your attention to some other, higher need.

When we've basically satisfied those four lower levels of need, Maslow theorized, we're free to address the highest level, the need for self-actualization. This is the need to fulfill your potential, to "be all you can be," to become the most complete individual you can become. Self-actualizers are the people who are truly happy, who are fulfilled in their lives, who are the most creative and productive.

Unfortunately, Maslow believed that just satisfying the D-needs is such a time-consuming struggle for the vast majority of human beings that only two percent of us ever manage to be self-actualizers.

I strongly disagree with Maslow on that point. Many more of us can achieve self-fulfillment than a mere two out of a hundred. But he's right that it's not easy. And he's right that you cannot achieve self-actualization as long as you are distracted by what he would call lesser needs.

Luckily, we live in a country where most of us can satisfy the majority of Maslow's D-needs with relative ease, compared to people in many other societies. Except for the very poor and the homeless, most of us have enough to eat, a roof over our heads, and so on. Yes, we have daily obligations, responsibilities, bills to pay. Still, despite its flaws, our society gives us extraordinary freedom to pursue higher goals. In this country, *you* are the only one holding you back from achieving your dreams. You have to search inside yourself and find those things that are going to make you truly happy.

Distinguishing Wants from Needs

The way I describe this process of search and discovery is that **you have to divide the world between wants and needs.**

Wants are those things that are literally not necessary to your happiness and do not actually build your happiness, even though they may be decorative to your life. That's very different from truly understanding what your needs are as a human being. Maybe it's to express yourself as an artist. Maybe it's to be an athlete. Maybe it's to go into business. Maybe it's surrounding yourself with children, like a schoolteacher. Maybe it's being the best parent you can possibly be, and experiencing all the riches (*not* money) and joys that come from raising a family well.

Whatever it is, you have to be realistic about the fact that it may have nothing to do with making money, or with what you do to make money.

I have a good friend, a really sweet woman, who's been in marketing her whole life. She hates it. She's an athlete at heart and she loves children; she loves teaching them sports. Many times

I've said to her, "Well, then why don't you become a coach?" But the combination of the money she makes and the "status" of being an executive in a marketing firm has kept her from self-actualizing. She's divided her life between the ten hours a day she spends on the job and the rest of her life where she's a happy mom playing sports with her kids. There's a ten-hour stretch every day where she's doing nothing to grow as a human being. She has the same complaints today as when I met her ten years ago.

Many people have segmented their lives this way. Think of that publicist I mentioned before, Dan Klores. Busy, successful, powerful, making good money—but in his heart and in his mind he was really a filmmaker. And as long as he kept repressing that filmmaker inside of him, no amount of success as a publicist was going to make him feel truly fulfilled and satisfied as a person.

When you're able to separate your wants from your true needs, and you can look inside for what's going to make you happy as opposed to the often false markers of happiness that society offers—the luxury car, the good neighborhood, all those wants that can influence your lifestyle—then you can begin to create a situation where your lifestyle flows from what truly makes you happy inside.

Our consumerist society does not make this easy for any of us. It can be extremely difficult to turn your attention away from the distracting and distorting *imagery of need* that this society subjects us all to. I alluded to this above. I'm talking about *the substitution of material attainment for spiritual attainment*.

In my career in advertising, I participated in this process myself. I worked early in my career on a Coca-Cola account, a soft drink called Mellow Yellow. It's like Mountain Dew, and it's sold in the Midwest and the South. Our data showed that most people who drink Mellow Yellow are blue-collar workers. So we did a beautiful commercial, in which we showed a construction site, with rugged, sweaty construction workers having a refreshing Mellow Yellow as a pretty girl walks by. It flopped miserably. When the target audience was shown that, they saw their lives—and they rejected it. They didn't *want* to see their lives. We had to change the imagery. Not the message—this is a refreshing soda, you'll attract pretty girls if you drink it—just the imagery. So the next commercial, which was wildly successful, showed two guys, similar to the ones in the first commercial, only now they were in a cool 1960s convertible, driving through the desert, stopping for a drink, and meeting the sexy women there.

Essentially, what we had to do was project the imagery of desire—put the target audience's desires on the screen—so that when they bought Mellow Yellow they felt they were also buying into that desired lifestyle.

That's the sort of technique used by the advertising and marketing community to *create patterns of need*. And in doing so they have created a distortion of wants and needs. My son, who is three and a half, watches children's programs on TV. He'll see ten commercials, and after eight of them turn to my wife and me and say, "I *need* that." That's the technique at work. Obviously, he doesn't *need* any of the things in those ads.

But that's what this society does: It replaces values like love and true satisfaction with consumption. And for many of us, that has distorted the relationship between wants and needs. And it is impossible to become truly happy if you cannot differentiate between the two.

Further confusing people is the way this society equates acquiring and consuming goods with social status. Status is directly tied to the type of car you drive, the watch you wear. We don't simply acquire these things, we feel the need to show them off to everyone else. Like other primates, we're obsessively status-conscious. We all want to know where we fit in the tribal hierarchy, and we want everyone else—or at least those below us—to know it, too. We show our social position by flashing our expensive watches, our jewelry, our fancy cars.

That kind of ostentatious display got Julius Caesar killed. In republican Rome, aristocratic men displayed their coveted senate membership by wearing togas with a single purple stripe running down them. One of the reasons Caesar was assassinated is that he insisted on wearing a toga that was all purple, making others highly jealous and angry.

The first critical factor when you're trying to identify what will make you truly happy and then set your sights on how to achieve that is to *separate money from the equation.* Yes, you'll have to deal with the realities of your life. If you're a parent with three children and all the responsibilities that entails, you can't wake up one morning and decide, "I'm going to quit my job and go be an artist." But if you don't develop this ongoing process of self-analysis and learn how to separate your wants from your needs, you'll never realize your true happiness.

FIND YOUR OWN MOUNTAINTOP

No, it's not easy to tell the difference between what you simply want and what you truly need. You need to analyze and be honest with yourself about what is important and what is going to drive you. My whole life is a process of self-analysis. Most of my waking day is focused on sequencing: What do I want to accomplish? What's the process? What's the impact of what I do on what I ultimately hope to achieve? It's a constant questioning of what I truly need to do and what really drives me.

A lot of people simply don't know what they really want to do with their lives and their talents. They don't know that they really want to be a filmmaker or a teacher or an athletic coach.

In the attitude of silence the soul finds the path in a clearer light, and what is elusive and deceptive resolves itself into crystal clearness.

—MAHATMA GANDHI

They spend their entire lives searching for some sense of fulfillment, but they'll never find it because they haven't identified what it is they're actually seeking.

Sometimes it takes some terrible crisis in our lives, a tragic and traumatic event, to shock us into thinking more clearly about who we are and what we should be doing with our lives. A loved one dies, and the shock of that death makes us think more closely about our own life. "What if I were to die tomorrow?" we think. "What will I have accomplished in my life?"

For me, it wasn't such a tragic event as the loss of a loved one, but it was still a moment of personal crisis. It occurred when I got that promotion at AT&T that I mentioned, after working like a maniac for it and thinking that was what I wanted. When I got that promotion, I suddenly realized it had nothing to do with my true self or where I wanted to go in my life. As self-aware as I like to think I am, I still had a hard time understanding that. I had to go to that mountaintop in Nepal to figure it out.

But you don't need to wait for a life crisis to begin assessing your true self and real needs, and you don't have to go to Nepal to take that journey of understanding and self-knowledge. Ultimately, it's an *inner* journey. Joseph Campbell said, "Your sacred space is where you can find yourself again and again." By sacred space he meant precisely the mental state I'm discussing here. There's that mountaintop in everyone's life, and in yours, too: a place or state of mind where you can filter out the distractions, correct the distortions, and analyze your wants and needs with clarity. Nirvana is not a place, but a mind-set.

For some people it's intense exercise at the gym, or thirty minutes a day of yoga and deep breathing. For others it's spending an hour a day reading the books that could influence their lives; it could be the Bible, or biographies of successful role models. Maybe it's gardening, a long walk or jog, or a bike ride. Maybe it's going to a park, a museum, a church.

Where is that quiet space for you? Find that place where you can cancel out the buzzing distractions of everyday life—your job, the telephone, the television, the unpaid bills, even your family—just for an hour or two, even if it's only a couple of times a week, and listen to your inner voice, examine your core desires and needs.

Finding that mechanism, your personal vehicle for taking that inner trip of discovery, is key.

REVIEW

- Success is finding that vocation in your life that allows you to be the finest person you can be. Success is being able to look back and realize that for each stage of your life, you were able to achieve the most that you could.

- Success doesn't just happen to people. You have to make your own success. You have to make your own luck.

- Success is not money. Money will not buy you happiness.

- You cannot consume happiness from outside. Happiness has to come from inside. Happiness is not passive. It is active. It is not a material object you can acquire or eat or own. It is a state of being you create.

- Don't put off your quest for happiness to some distant, theoretical future. That time may never come. Begin your journey now.

- Search inside yourself to discover what truly makes you happy. Make the distinction between what you merely want and what you truly need to in order to be fulfilled.

EXERCISE: Dividing Wants from Needs

There are those things we acquire to fulfill our basic needs for food, shelter, and clothing. Then there are those things we buy because we hope somehow they'll make us happier. All of us, rich or poor, are encouraged to try to buy our way to happiness. A vacation house, a sporty second car, a big TV or stereo, flashy jewelry—whatever we can afford (and, often, even if we can't afford it).

The funny thing is, having these objects rarely makes us as happy as we expected them to. Psychologists have actually studied the difference between how happy we think having these things will make us, and their real impact on our lives. They've even given it a label, "affective forecasting."

Try this exercise. Below, list the last five objects you acquired because you thought having them would truly make your life happier and more fulfilled. Not necessities like food or the roof over your head, but the gold watch, the bigger TV, the louder stereo. Whatever they were, list them here:

1. _____
2. _____
3. _____
4. _____
5. _____

First ask yourself: *Did any of these objects really make me a happier or more fulfilled human being?* Be honest.

Now put it to the test. What if you were forced to give up one of these objects? Pick which of the five you'd be most willing to live without if you had to, and cross it off your list.

Now you've got only four items. Are you any less of a person?

Imagine you were forced to give up one of those four objects. Pick one and cross it off. Now you have only three left. Are you really only three-fifths as happy as you were before?

What if you had to eliminate one of those three items? Cross it off. You're down to two.

Now pick one of those and cross it off.

What's left? Presumably, it's the one object of the five that you believe is most essential to your personal happiness.

(continued)

Now cross that one out too.

All gone. The watch, the stereo, the sports car, the big TV.

Now think about this carefully: *What do you have left?* You've still got the roof over your head, clothing, food. You've still got your dreams and hopes, your passionate interests, your skills and talents, *your life* and all the possibilities and potential it represents.

Aren't these the things that truly make you happy? Imagine if you were asked to list these things—my health, my family, my friends, and so on—and then told to start crossing them off, one by one.

That's one way to distinguish between wants and needs.

EXERCISE: Your Own Personal Mountaintop

I went on a literal trip, my trip to that mountaintop in Nepal, to find the space and time to figure out my life's mission. But you don't have to travel to take that journey of understanding and self-knowledge. Ultimately, it's an *inner* journey.

There are places, times, or activities that will allow you to filter out the distractions and demands of your daily life, so that you can focus inwardly and think clearly about who you truly are and what you really need to do with your life. Quiet times when you can examine your core self, determine what you want to accomplish, and plan how to go about that. Maybe it's thirty minutes a day of yoga or karaoke spinning at the gym. Maybe it's a grassy spot in the sun on your lunch break. Maybe it's a walk through the Museum of Trains and Automobiles. Or maybe it's climbing into bed and finally reading *Don Quixote*.

Below, list those spaces, times, or activities in your life:

1. _____
2. _____
3. _____
4. _____
5. _____

Now make a schedule to visit that quiet place on a regular basis. Be realistic about coming up with a schedule you'll be able to keep, whether that's thirty minutes a day after work, or an hour a week, or whatever you can manage. And begin to visit that private mountaintop as soon and as often as you reasonably can.

PRINCIPLE TWO

Set Goals and Be Flexible

Why not go out on a limb?
That's where the fruit is.

— WILL ROGERS

WHO ARE YOU REALLY?

Many of us, especially in America, when asked, "Who are you?" will initially respond as though we were asked, "What do you do?" We'll say, "I'm a security guard at a bank," "I clean offices in a large building," "I develop software," and so on. We respond as though our job or our financial status or something else about our current situation is what defines who we are.

There are people who truly are fulfilling themselves through their work. And it has nothing to do with how much money or status their jobs afford them. That bartender I mentioned in chapter 1, the teacher who's devoted his life to helping teens in the detention center get their GEDs, the gifted florist who opens her own shop and makes each arrangement a unique work of art—they're in all walks of life.

Still, many of us find ourselves in jobs we've taken out of a sense of financial necessity, or just because we've never thought very seriously about doing anything else. Our current jobs are what we *do,* but they're not who we *are.* You're not really a grocery store cashier, a security guard, or a junior executive at an insurance firm. That's what you do to make a living, and there's absolutely nothing dishonorable or "wrong" about that, but it doesn't define you as a human being.

No one knows this better than people in the arts in America. In most New York City and Los Angeles restaurants, there's a good chance that your waiter or waitress is a struggling young actor. If you ask them who they are, they'll tell you, "I'm an actor. I'm only waiting tables until I get my big break." Of course, they won't *all* get that big break, but at least they're clear that what they're doing to pay the rent is not who they are. There's even a fingernail polish called "I'm Not Really a Waitress."

There is a key difference between an *occupation* and a *vocation*. Many people confuse the two. Our occupations are our jobs—what we do to make money to live and pay our bills. Our vocations are our higher callings: the thing or things in life that truly define who we are. Some people are fortunate enough to have their vocation be their occupation as well. Most of us need to realize this distinction and separate *what we do* from *who we are.*

I know a painter who for years made his living as a waiter. He wasn't bad at waiting tables, but he didn't much care about it, either. It was just what he did so he could afford to keep painting. One time he was working in a restaurant when the maître d' took him aside and told him somberly, "I'm sorry, but I'm going to have to let you go. I don't know how to tell you this, Rick, but you're no waiter." Rick thought about that a second, smiled broadly, and said, "Thanks!"

In the introduction I described how I've been working since I was in the sixth grade, when I pumped gas at a filling station. I worked all through junior high, high school, and college, and graduated straight into the working world. From pumping gas to cleaning out pet cages to delivering Chinese food, I don't regret having worked any of those jobs. I learned things about the world and about myself at every one of them.

But did any of them define me as a person? No. They were occupations, not vocations. Who I truly was was never a dishwasher or soda jerk, or even a managing director at Ogilvy & Mather. And that's true for a lot of people. When asked, "But I mean who are you *really*?" that branch manager may say, "Well, I'm a bank branch manager, but my *real passion* is photography"—just as Rick would say, "I'm an artist," or the successful publicity agent knew that he was really a documentary filmmaker. Many of us have this other, often secret self inside us—the true self, whom we repress and frustrate, or whom we may not even have discovered yet. We've let our jobs, our bills, our social status, the needs and expectations of others define who we are externally; we allow our occupations to eclipse our true vocations. Often that person we seem to be on the outside, the one we present to the world and even to our friends and loved ones, has very little to do with who we truly are inside.

When you've found your own mountaintop, that quiet space where you can filter out all the external influences and distractions of your life and turn your focus inward, you can begin to reacquaint yourself with that inner you, the true you. Because you're alone with your thoughts, you can be completely honest with yourself. There's no one else on your mountaintop—not your boss or coworkers, not your friends, or even your family—to disagree or be upset with your answers to questions like "Who am I really? What is my vocation?" and "What would truly make me feel like I was fulfilling my potential as a human being?" You're free to answer honestly: I'm really a filmmaker. I'm a ballerina. I'm an entrepreneur. I'm an inspiring teacher. I'm a nurturing mother. I'm an organic farmer.

Obviously, though, simply saying to yourself that you *want* to be a ballerina or an astronaut isn't the end of this journey. In fact, it's only the first step. What if you're deluding yourself? What if all you've really identified is not your true self but merely a lifelong daydream or fantasy?

The next step is to analyze the goal you've identified. Is this who I really am? Is this what I really want to do? You must test the hypothesis by asking yourself some more questions and answering them as clearly as possible. Some of those questions include:

1. Why do I believe this will truly fulfill me as a person?

2. Do I have the necessary basic skills and talents?

3. What other skills must I acquire? How can I do that?

4. Can I fulfill other necessary requirements?

If your goal is to be a major-league pitcher, but you're forty-five years old and haven't thrown a fastball since you were on your high school varsity team, answering questions 2 and 4 honestly will tell you that you're too old and too long out of training.

Similarly, let's say you're a thirty-year-old, 150-pound, working mother with two children, and your goal is to be a prima ballerina. An honest self-assessment is going to indicate that this is also a highly unlikely prospect for you. Ballerinas begin training in their childhood, and train very hard, every day of their lives. They devote themselves obsessively to the ballet. They're also well under 150 pounds. The Bolshoi recently fired a ballerina for being overweight—at 109 pounds!

I offer those two examples because they're both representative of a syndrome that holds a lot of adults back from thinking clearly about what would truly make them happy: *the unwillingness to let go of childhood fantasies.* Being a major league pitcher is a schoolboy's dream; becoming a prima ballerina is a girl's. They're common answers to "What do you want to be when you grow up?"

It's fine to want to be a pitcher, a ballerina, an astronaut, or a movie star when you're eight years old. It's something else entirely to be holding on to those dreams when you're twenty-eight or thirty-eight and have not developed the applicable skills.

If you're in the middle of your life, you may need to face the fact that those opportunities passed you by, for whatever reason. Is holding on to those dreams the best use of your life at this point? Aren't you just putting off finding your true self? What good is it to visualize a self that you can't achieve, then say, "Well, if I can't be a ballerina, I don't care what I do." It's a way to let yourself off the hook psychologically—an excuse not to think seriously about your goals and your potentials at this stage in your life.

We all live our lives in stages. Who you were, what you dreamed of accomplishing and what you could achieve when you were in grade school is very different from who you are and what you can achieve in your mid-thirties. And that's different from who you will be at sixty-five. Part of the process of discovering your true self is to let go of antiquated ideas about yourself, prejudices you have about what you can and can't do, what you want and don't want to achieve.

Please understand: I am not saying that you can ever be too old to have dreams and goals and reach for them. My wife's grandmother learned to play the violin at eighty-six. At eighty-eight, she learned how to write her poetry on a personal computer. No one would have told her it was realistic for her to think she could do those things at her age. She didn't let that stop her.

That's very different from the forty-five-year-old pitcher and the thirty-year-old ballerina. My wife's grandmother's goals were achievable, even at her advanced stage in life. Theirs are probably not. Had she decided to become a ballerina instead of learning the violin, that would be a different matter.

We all know of people who seem to have dreams that are not only unrealistic but downright ridiculous. Think of the contestants who audition for the popular TV show *American Idol.* In the first round, all sorts of hopefuls audition before a three-judge panel; if they pass, they're invited to Hollywood for the next round. For some of these first-round contestants, the dream of stardom is so obviously disconnected from their actual level of talent that it's painful to watch. These people have invested their lives in the dream of becoming a recording star, and some of them can't hold a note.

I would suggest that these are people who haven't really gone through a process of determining their real desires and true goals. They seem to have decided that they "need" to be rich and famous pop stars, to be surrounded by fans and admirers. Of course, they don't really require that. What they need to do is fulfill themselves as human beings. They're hardly going to do that by making fools of themselves on national television. For them to enter this talent contest is the equivalent of hoping to win the lottery: It's an "easy," get-rich-quick scheme, not a real-life mission. They need to analyze their wants and needs carefully.

Both the wanna-be pitcher and the would-be ballerina need to do this, too. An honest self-assessment should convince them to adjust their sights. They may not necessarily need to abandon their interest in sports or dance altogether. The forty-five-year-old may find some fulfillment coaching Little League, for instance. The thirty-year-old mother can still get involved in dance-related activities. She could try volunteering in the office of a dance company. Or go back to school and get a degree in dance therapy.

But they both need to do some rigorous, honest analysis of those childhood dreams to see how relevant they are to their lives as adults. And if those dreams are childish fantasies that are preventing them from actively seeking happiness, they need to abandon them.

CHOOSE YOUR OWN PATH

Two roads diverged, in a wood, and I—
I took the one less traveled by,
And that has made all the difference.

— ROBERT FROST

Many people look to others to make them happy. In its way, this is as distracting as looking to money to make you happy. You have to do it for yourself. **Only you can develop your own sense of your worth. Only you can identify your goal and travel your path toward happiness and success.** No one else can do it for you.

Too many people live their lives passively. They just drift through life day to day, reacting to what the world brings them. That kind of reactive way of living is a recipe for reaching your sixties or seventies and suddenly finding you've got very little to point to in the way of what you've accomplished with your life. How sad to say, "This was my journey. Was this all I was able to achieve?" The urgency of taking this moment to begin the process of self-analysis and discovery can't be overstated. There may be no tomorrow. Each day you delay your process of self-realization is a wasted day, and those are potentially adding up to a wasted life—because you don't know how long your life's going to be, how long you're going to be around.

Joseph Campbell, the great scholar of world cultures and religions, pointed out that the idea of your life as a journey is one that people around the world have embraced. In many cultures there are very precise "initiation" rituals to mark the moment in an adolescent's life when childhood ends and that young person takes the first step on the path of adulthood. It's a journey each individual must take for himself or herself, along a path that he or she alone follows.

We have some similar initiation rites in our society. Among Jews, there's the bar mitzvah (for boys) and bat mitzvah (for girls). For Roman Catholics, confirmation serves the same basic ritual purpose. And yet our society does not always encourage us to choose our own path in life. We are far more often expected simply to accept some role that has already been created for us— to join a large corporation, for example, or "marry well." We are encouraged to be followers or members of the team rather than leaders and innovators. We are often expected to be passive and content with what life hands us, rather than to be creative and proactive about making our own lives as rich and fulfilling as they can be.

Simply following a life path that has been handed to you by others is not the route to a successful or happy life. You can only achieve true success and real happiness by examining your own needs, setting your own goals, and then following your own path.

You may know something of the old tales regarding the Knights of the Round Table and the Holy Grail. To storytellers in the Middle Ages, the Grail was the chalice Jesus used at the Last Supper, one of the most sacred objects in all Christianity. Its whereabouts were shrouded in mystery. To find and acquire the Grail represented the highest level of spiritual achievement.

The knights of King Arthur's Round Table set out to find the Grail and bring it to Camelot. It was the most holy and noble quest they could imagine. When the knights set out on this quest, they thought it would be a disgrace if they all set out in a group together; each individual knight had to go alone, and follow his own path, in the hopes of finding the Grail. And so, when they came to the edge of a vast, dense forest in which the Grail was thought to be hidden, each knight entered the woods alone, at a spot where no one had created a previous path or track. While making his way through the forest, if a knight came upon the trail of another, he did not follow it; the ones who followed a path already created by another knight were inevitably led astray, away from the Grail, away from their goal. By following his own individual path, despite all the fear and obstacles that path may have presented him, each knight brought about his own unique outcome.

I believe that life is like that for each and every one of us. If you do not follow your own path, you will never find your personal Grail of success and happiness—and like each of the knights, your own path to success is totally individual, totally unique. Yes, the woods are dark and deep and frightening and filled with obstacles and challenges. But the rewards of following your own path through those woods are immense.

Something else that may hold people back from even trying to achieve their goal are their duties and responsibilities to others. You have a spouse, you have a daughter who seems to go through three pairs of sneakers a month, you have to scrape together the mortgage every four weeks. You can't just come home from work one day and tell your family, "I quit my job. I'm going to pursue my true goal and become a ballerina."

But I'm telling you, you cannot be a good father, mother, son, or daughter unless you are truly happy yourself. So **finding your true self, being on the path of self-actualization, is the biggest gift you can give—not just to yourself but to everyone around you.** Your obligations to others might mean that you have to choose a different path to happiness than you would have if you were alone in the world. It might mean you can't just quit your job and go learn how to be a painter or a ballerina. You might have to parcel it into smaller steps. But in the end, not following your plan for self-actualization is the path to destruction—not just your own destruction but possibly the destruction of your marriage and other relationships.

You have to believe in yourself and your vision. This belief begins with the process of self-analysis and discovering who you want to be and what it is that ultimately you want to do, understanding your vocation. Then, when you've identified what you truly need to do to fulfill yourself as a human being, you have to trust yourself and have faith in that vision, even if it seems "unrealistic." If you've performed your self-audit honestly, then your goal is not unrealistic, no matter how far off it may seem. You have to have faith that your true self is not, for example, a public relations man, even with all the money and power that brings you. Dan Klores knew in his heart that he really was a filmmaker. To actualize that knowledge, he had to believe he was a filmmaker before he ever picked up a camera. If it's truly what's at the core of you as a person, and your self-analysis has shown you that this is something you can achieve, then the very first step in your personal transformation is the belief that in fact this is what you're meant to be and it is who you are. Then, you can transform your situation to make the outside world conform to that inner reality.

The unactualized human is a bitter, dangerous being. The psychologist Abraham Maslow, who theorized the hierarchy of needs discussed in chapter 1, argued that what we call "evil" behavior—destructiveness, sadism, cruelty, malice, and so on— are symptoms of the gnawing, soul-deep dissatisfaction and frustration we feel when we are not meeting our higher needs. This may show itself in relatively harmless ways. Or, as we see every day in our society, it can turn someone into a vicious individual who strikes out, either in large ways—violent criminal behavior—or in petty ways—the store clerk who refuses to look you in the eye, the driver who cuts you off on the highway, the corporate drone who revels in making things difficult for everyone else. Do not frustrate your dream. You will never find real happiness or true success that way.

STRATEGY AND TACTICS

If one does not know to which port one is sailing, no wind is favorable.

—SENECA

Envisioning your future and then plotting a course toward it entail both *strategic* and *tactical* thinking. Lots of people are confused about the difference between strategy and tactics. In simplest terms, strategy means overarching, broad-strokes planning. Tactics refers to the steps within that strategy that cause the broader plan to happen. In military terms, strategic planning refers to why and how you plan to win the entire war; tactics is how you plan and execute each of the battles that add up to that final victory.

Some people are good only at strategic thinking, others only at tactics. Strategic thinkers may be great at having the big vision, the broad stroke of genius, but cannot bring themselves to do the day-to-day tactical planning that's going to get them to that larger goal. They get frustrated because they can see that larger goal so clearly and can't understand why they can't make it all happen right now, without bothering with all the boring little steps along the way.

Other people are great at working out the day-to-day tactical details of their lives but have no sense of the greater picture, no clear, ideal understanding of what their strategic goal is or where their life is taking them. They just get by from day to day to day, basically reacting to what each day brings. They may not experience terrible unhappiness from one day to the next—after all, they're getting by, they're coping, they'll let the future take care of itself. But they still feel frustrated because they're aware, even if it's only a vague sense of uneasiness and dissatisfaction, that their lives should have more meaning and add up to something more than just the daily details. The problem is, they have no idea of what that larger goal is.

I recently saw an unfortunate example of bad strategic and tactical planning. There was a happy couple in their thirties. He designed and built commercial spaces like stores and restaurants. She was an excellent cook, and they were both passionate "foodies." He had just completed construction of a beautiful new restaurant. When he went to collect his fee, however, the owners told him they had run out of money. Not only were they unable to open the restaurant, but they couldn't pay him for building it, either. (These people were obviously bad tactical planners themselves!) In lieu of cash, they offered to give him the restaurant.

He and his wife had often dreamed of having a restaurant of their own—the kind of nouvelle cuisine restaurant where they themselves loved to eat, with a boldly inventive menu and an excellent wine list and all the "foodie" trimmings. They had never seriously thought it would happen. Now fate seemed to be handing them a golden opportunity. They knew they'd be taking an enormous leap into the dark. Neither of them had any experience in the restaurant business. And they were aware that restaurants are among the most risky of all small businesses; a huge percentage of new restaurants fail in the first year. But this seemed to them a once-in-a-lifetime opportunity they simply could not refuse.

You had to admire their courage and their willingness to take the leap. And when they opened the restaurant, it was indeed the kind of establishment they'd always dreamed of: gorgeously designed, an ingenious young chef, and so on.

But they struggled from the day it opened, and were forced to close within a year.

Why? One reason was that they proved to be poor strategists. They didn't do their homework. It turned out that people who went out to eat in the neighborhood where the restaurant was located didn't *like* nouvelle cuisine or inventive menus, and couldn't tell a good wine from a bad one. All they knew was that the good ones were too expensive. They liked modest, old-fashioned spaghetti restaurants and steakhouses. Many of them were senior citizens who flocked to restaurants that opened early and offered discounted "early-bird specials." They were far more interested in getting a doggy-bag-sized meal at a modest price than having an expensively novel dining experience. They wanted a glass of the house red filled to the rim, not an inch of an exquisite Bordeaux in a balloon snifter. This new place was simply too fancy, too experimental for the neighborhood.

The owners could have predicted all this. Visiting the successful restaurants in the area and doing a bit of research on the neighborhood's demographics could have told them all they needed to know. Then they could either have adapted their dream to the neighborhood realities to give it a better chance of succeeding—that is, changed their strategy, or opted out of the project altogether. Once the restaurant was open and struggling, they had another opportunity to adapt. They could have been more flexible about the menu and the wine list, maybe offered some discount enticements to draw the locals in—that is, changed their tactics. But that didn't fit their vision.

Again, you have to give them credit for having the courage of their convictions. But in the end, that unwillingness to bend doomed the enterprise. They succeeded in envisioning and creating the restaurant, but failed utterly in the strategic vision for their neighborhood and the pragmatic tactics that might have helped make it a success.

Understanding the need for both strategic and tactical thinking is a fundamental step in the planning process. You must be able to first visualize your goal strategically, then map out the tactical steps that will lead you to it.

Start out literally drawing a map or a list on a sheet of paper: "This is where I want to go, and these are the steps."

Let's pick an easy example. I'm a young person and I want to become a physician. What are the basic steps to get there? Well, I need:

- good high school grades that will get me into college

- four years of undergraduate study

- four years of medical school

- two years of residency

But our goals aren't always so simply defined. Perhaps my goal is to get married. Easily said, but finding the right mate is far more difficult. If my strategy is to meet my soul mate, what are the tactical steps that will lead me there? Clearly, I can't simply sit at home and wait for Mr. or Ms. Right to knock on the door. I need to get out and about, to put myself in situations where I'll meet other singles. I take my sheet of paper and I start brainstorming and jotting down ideas.

One tactic might simply be to go out to more parties.

Another might be to join a church group, finally bite the bullet, and show up at the Friday-night "Rockin' With the Lord" party.

Another might be to join some clubs or other organizations that both match my interests and will put me in situations where I'll meet other singles. For example, I like to dance; perhaps I should join one of those groups where people meet one night a week to practice swing dancing or square dancing or the tango.

Another might be to avail myself of some of the many singles dating services on the Internet.

As you're making this list, it may become obvious that other incremental or preliminary steps are needed. For instance, it might not do you much good to be out in public if you're so painfully shy you'll never speak to anyone. You may need to take some confidence-building steps first—a course in public speaking, perhaps, or an acting class.

I knew a woman in her thirties, Laurie, who was in desperate financial straits. She was a single mother raising a ten-year-old daughter and struggling just to make the rent each month. She was a skilled photographer, a good writer, a former actress and model—an impressive package of skills, looks, and intelligence, but unfortunately not a very marketable one in a depressed economy when you're a single mother and having to pick your child up every day after school at three P.M. She was job hunting like crazy and would interview for anything—baby-sitting, waitressing, receptionist, computer data entry. But Laurie was trapped in a complicated catch-22. Either employers thought she was wildly overqualified for the position, or the job's hours would require her to pay for child care, which would eat up most of what she was earning.

When you're in that kind of a desperate situation, it can be extremely difficult to think about a long-term strategy for achieving your Grail. All your time and energy and ingenuity are taken up by immediate needs and problems. But these can also be the times when it's most beneficial psychologically to have a greater goal for your life, beyond the day-to-day headaches and worries. It's a source of power to be able to say, "This may be where I am today, but it's not where I'm going to be tomorrow," even if "tomorrow" is five or ten years down the path. Having a long-term plan can help you deal with short-term problems.

Asked what she really wanted to do with her life, Laurie replied quickly that she'd most like to combine her experience as a photographer, a writer, and an actress: She wanted to be a film-maker. For a single mother in her situation, this might seem an utterly "unrealistic" goal. But rather than simply giving up, she worked backward from that seemingly unattainable goal and visualized the incremental, tactical steps she could take on the path that might eventually get her there.

She decided that the first step was to reestablish herself as a professional photographer. Okay, how to do that? First she needed to reorganize her portfolio of photographs, with new prints of her best shots. Then she could begin to take that around to the agencies and photographers' representatives who might find her work. The catch was that it would cost as much as $5,000 to have professional-quality prints made of her color photographs. In her position, $5,000 might as well have been $500,000.

She decided to concentrate on her black-and-white photos instead—those she could print herself. But there was yet another catch: She had no darkroom or equipment. She found out that there were professional darkroom facilities in her city that she could rent by the hour. It might cost her more like $500 rather than $5,000 to rebuild her portfolio that way. Without new color prints it wouldn't be the ideal portfolio, but it would be enough to get her in the door at those agencies. In her financial state, $500 was still a large amount, but she didn't need to come up with it in one lump sum. She could rent the darkroom an hour or two at a time, at $20 an hour, and rebuild her portfolio in small, affordable increments.

Obviously, Laurie was not going to become a filmmaker overnight. She might never attain that goal. But by breaking up the path toward that goal into small, realizable steps, she saw that she could take positive action and slowly begin to realize her goal, rather than simply give up before the enormity of her "unrealistic" dream. And these were small steps she could take even while continuing to struggle to find work, raise her child, and pay the rent every month. It wouldn't be easy—it would, in fact, be difficult as hell—but it was doable. It may not lead her to her ultimate goal, but it would lead *somewhere*—somewhere positive.

The great psychologist Alfred Adler (some people argue that he, not Sigmund Freud, is the true "father of psychology") stressed the importance of having a future goal as a way of coping with the trials you may be experiencing in the present. "By means of this concrete goal," he wrote, "the individual can think and feel himself superior to the difficulties of the present because he has in mind his success of the future." The psychological uplift our photographer derived from having a goal and a road map toward it helped her cope with depressing day-to-day circumstances. Despair and hopelessness are the enemies of us all. A goal and a plan are powerful weapons in combating despair.

When you discover who your true self is, that can become a powerful beacon that guides you through your dark periods. This beacon is always on, and you can always orient yourself by its light. Even in moments of great despair, you hear a little voice inside of you that says, "I'm not a broken person who can't pay the rent next month. I'm actually a filmmaker."

By visualizing your success and prioritizing steps that lead you to your goals, even the most daunting tasks become manageable.

TACTICAL SHIFTS AND COURSE CORRECTIONS

Every future reality is made up of component parts: events you've lived, things you've done to get there, situations you put yourself in. Planning is a matter of deconstructing the future to see what those parts are. It's a tricky exercise, because by definition we don't know what the future will bring. And you can't force the future, either. So while you're planning the steps, you need to have a certain flexibility about it.

Flexibility is important for two reasons. First, events will occur that you didn't plan for. You have to be open-minded and ready to take advantage of new, unplanned opportunities when they materialize, and be able to incorporate them into your vision. We'll look at this more closely in the next chapter.

Then there's the opposite phenomenon: I call it the seven-ton piano falling on your head. Everything's going well, you've done everything you're supposed to do, and suddenly disaster strikes out of nowhere. Everything changes at that point. My parents' divorce was a seven-ton piano falling on my head when I was a kid. Later, StarMedia was sailing along brilliantly when suddenly the bottom dropped out of the Internet at the same time the Latin American economy flagged. We were going to interconnect all of Latin America, and then the seven-ton piano fell on us. You can only do so much. There's an extent to which you can't control events and all your best planning is subject to larger forces operating in the world.

Those pianos can fall out of the sky on all of us. In the last few years, as the world economy has lurched and contracted, many of us suddenly found ourselves out of a job, and all our best-laid plans—the money we were saving for a retirement home at the beach or to put a child through college, the addition we were going to build on the house, whatever it was—abruptly looked like impossible dreams. Or a sudden illness strikes you down. Or divorce.

Those sorts of lightning reversals of fortune are an integral part of life. But how you deal with them is also a crucial factor in whether you're going to find your success in life over time. All successful people have had seven-ton pianos fall on them. How they dealt with those moments of crisis, how they adjusted to the setbacks and adapted to new realities, is a big part of what made them successful.

Please note that I am not talking about a stoic inflexibility in the face of all adversity. That tough-guy, stiff-upper-lip, John Wayne figure marching grimly forward in the face of all opposition is a popular one—and misleading and even dangerous. In real life, it's the stiff, inflexible John Wayne characters who most often are the worst at dealing with sudden changes of fortune, who can't adapt their plans to get around some unforeseen obstacle, who find it the hardest to get up after some stroke of bad luck has knocked them down.

The supple willow bends before the stiff wind that uproots the mighty oak.

Successful people develop an attitude toward life that accepts and incorporates the fact that the occasional seven-ton piano will fall on their heads. They know to expect that crises will occur. They have a goal, but they're able to adapt as situations develop. They understand that moments of crisis are also moments of growth. These are moments when you can learn something about yourself. They're opportunities to rethink your planning and reinvent yourself.

There's more than one path toward your desired future. You have to be ready, willing, and open-minded to take a new path toward your goal when it presents itself. But never lose sight of that goal.

Of course, in some cases you may be focused on so narrow and specific a goal that its outcome depends only on you. You want to climb Mt. McKinley, or shave two minutes off your 6K Run for Fun time. But most goals are dependent on the actions of at least one other person. So being able to be the willow that bends rather than the oak that breaks—to be able to sway with the situation, and *enjoy* it—is very important. It's been said a thousand times, but it's true: It's not really the destination, it's the trip.

Every single day has its own goal, which is achieving some sense of accomplishment, happiness, or peace. The needs you have as a human being may be achieved in different ways at different stages in your life. Perhaps in this part of your life, keeping that job in advertising is a good thing. But that might not be the case three years from now. It's critical to balance the short term and the long term, to understand that sometimes the shortest path to your goal is not a straight line but one that goes through multiple deviations. Each of those deviations can be interesting of itself, and each adds to your life.

There's no better example of tactical flexibility in the service of a strategic goal than the life of Mahatma Gandhi. When Gandhi was born, in 1869, India was under British rule, the "jewel" of the British Empire. After an unremarkable middle-class childhood and undistinguished education, Gandhi traveled as a young lawyer to South Africa, where the raw racial prejudice and social inequities he witnessed ignited in him a passion for justice and freedom. He devoted the rest of his life to the service of humanity and literally transformed himself, becoming both a devout Hindu ascetic and an unstoppable force for social and political change. The tactics of nonviolent civil disobedience he developed, known as "passive resistance," would later profoundly influence Dr. Martin Luther King, Jr., and the civil rights movement in the United States. He is a transcendental hero to me.

From 1919 until his death in 1948, Gandhi led the nation of India in its successful quest for independence from British rule. He was less successful, unfortunately, in his simultaneous attempts to lead India on a moral and spiritual revival (though he himself is one of the greatest spiritual figures in history) and to unite India's warring Muslim and Hindu populations (the Muslims would soon split from India and create their own nation of Pakistan).

Gandhi's philosophy, and his strategy and tactics for achieving his very lofty goals, did not suddenly come to him in a blinding light of revelation. He developed his ideas and his tactics throughout his life, balancing his moral and spiritual goals with his more pragmatic political and social agendas. He was thus sometimes criticized for contradicting himself or for being "inconsistent." He happily admitted to this: "I am not at all concerned with appearing to be consistent," he once wrote. "In my search after Truth I have discarded many ideas and learnt many new things. . . . What I am concerned with is my readiness to obey the call of Truth, my God, from moment to moment . . ."

In other words, he was less interested in being *consistent* than he was in being *right*. He meant that **you have to be open to adjusting your tactics when the situation calls for it, even if it completely contradicts something you said or did before.** This was a man who had the grand vision of overthrowing the British Empire—certainly a "crazy" vision for its time. But he carried it through in his life's work, and he succeeded in part because he valued being right over being consistent.

In our society we often overvalue consistency. I'm not saying it's "bad" to be consistent—we correctly honor a consistently loving person, for example, or a consistently generous one. But in terms of how you guide your life, to follow through with a plan just for the sake of consistency, even after it becomes clear that you're on the wrong path, can be disastrous. Many people will stick to that wrong path simply because they don't want to appear inconsistent or frivolous. That's foolish.

Regarding the need for flexibility, I used to say to my management team, "We're facing a situation not unlike a nineteenth-century battle." They would nod, and I eventually realized they had no idea what I was talking about. "At the start, we decide the strategy for the battle. But then each general—each manager— has to go into the field. And because we don't have radios yet (it's the nineteenth century), and the fog of war is upon us, each general, as he's leading his troops, while keeping in mind the overarching strategy, has to go out and achieve his goal in the best way possible given the situation on the ground."

That's a metaphor for life. You can develop in your head the most elegant strategy for your life, but when you go into the field you have to go into what's been called "the fog of war." Life is like the fog of war. You have a lot less information than you'd like to have to make decisions about your life, but you have to decide anyway, you have to fight this battle regardless. And to do that you have to maintain flexibility, to understand that sometimes you have to go around a certain obstacle instead of through it. You may have to shift your short-term goals to achieve your long-term ones.

Alexander the Great is a fine example of a man who set the loftiest goals for himself and achieved them largely because of his skill for flexibility and adapting to different situations. His mother had raised him believing he was the son of Zeus himself, able to do whatever he pleased. He was only twenty-three when he became king of Macedonia in 336 B.C., and he had no clear long-term strategy for his reign at first. But he became passionately convinced that his destiny was to create an empire that would spread the influence and values of the Greek tradition throughout the known world, and he set out to do just that. By the time he died at the age of only thirty-two, he had created an empire so vast it was unthinkable in its day, encompassing most of the eastern Mediterranean, Egypt, Persia, and Asia Minor all the way to India. He defeated huge armies previously thought unbeatable, and incorporated an array of cultures and civilizations under his rule.

Alexander is still considered one of the greatest military geniuses in history. He achieved many of his most stunning victories through his ability to adapt to different battle scenarios and shift his tactics as needed. As a general he was unpredictable, wily, innovative, sometimes downright deceptive; he kept opposing generals off balance and bewildered with his impromptu battle plans. In his time (and to an extent this remained true all the way into the twentieth century), when large armies clashed, there were accepted formulas and traditions, almost a sort of choreography that both armies used in deploying their cavalry and foot soldiers. Much of Alexander's success was due to his ability to change the rules as needed in the midst of battle. He would misdirect, confuse, and mislead his more conservative enemies—and crush them. Sun Tsu, the great Chinese philosopher of war and Alexander's contemporary, wrote that one should "appear where your enemy does not expect you." Alexander did this brilliantly.

Tactical flexibility can make the difference between success and failure in your own life as well. Friends of mine were engaged to be married. Because they both lived in Brooklyn, they made arrangements to hold the ceremony on the pedestrian pathway of the beautiful Brooklyn Bridge. Unfortunately, the day of the wedding a torrential rainstorm blew in. Rather than panic and allow the weather to ruin the occasion, they remembered that under the Brooklyn side of the bridge is a large, vaulted space where an arts organization staged exhibitions. When they went there and explained their plight, the organization's staff was happy to help. The wedding went off at the appointed hour inside this handsome space, with art works in the background.

Bad weather was an obstacle my friends were powerless to change. But rather than let it prevent their happiness, they accepted the challenge, altered their plan, and found a creative solution. They had a joyous wedding—and have a great story to tell about that day as well.

Every day brings its own opportunities for happiness, and its own challenges. You can attain happiness every day if you're flexible and creative.

REVIEW

- There is a key difference between an *occupation* and a *vocation*. Our occupations are our jobs—what we do to make money to live and pay our bills. Our vocations are our higher callings: the thing or things in life that truly define who we are. Learn to distinguish between *what you do* and *who you are*.

- Don't look to others to make you happy. Only you can develop your own sense of your worth. Only you can identify your goal and travel your path toward happiness and success.

- Simply following a life path that has been handed to you by others is not the route to a successful or happy life. You can only achieve true success and real happiness by examining your own needs, setting your own goals, and then following your own path.

- The unactualized human is a bitter, dangerous being. Finding your true self, being on the path of self-actualization, is the biggest gift you can give—not just to yourself but to everyone around you.

- When you discover who your true self is, that can become a powerful beacon that guides you through your dark periods. By visualizing your success and prioritizing steps that lead you to your goals, even the most daunting tasks become manageable.

- Every single day has its own goal, which is achieving some sense of accomplishment, happiness, or peace. Every day brings its own opportunities for happiness, and its own challenges. You can attain happiness every day if you're flexible and creative.

EXERCISE: Who Am I Really?

For some people it's easy to say who they really are and what they want to do with their lives. They have no trouble distinguishing their current occupation from their true vocation. "I'm waiting tables, but what I really am is a dancer."

Others don't find answering these questions so easy. You may never have been encouraged to think about them seriously. You may not even know how to begin thinking about them.

Answering the questions below won't tell you "everything you need to know" about yourself. But it's a way to start thinking clearly about your vocation, your occupation, what makes you truly happy, and what you aspire to.

1. True or False: I feel that my current job or position makes me an asset to society.

2. True or False: I feel that my current job or position is as fulfilling to me as any job/position I could possibly imagine.

3. In remembering the past *month,* the following three events or moments made me the most happy:

    A. _____

    B. _____

    C. _____

    What do these events or moments seem to have in common?

    _____

    _____

4. In the past *year,* the following three events or moments made me the most happy:

    A. _____

    B. _____

    C. _____

    What do these events or moments seem to have in common?

    _____

    _____

(continued)

5. In thinking back, the five *worst* events/moments of my lifetime were:

A. _____

B. _____

C. _____

D. _____

E. _____

What do these events or moments seem to have in common?

_____

_____

6. In analyzing these positive and negative memories, I notice that I seem most to enjoy events or moments where I feel:

_____

_____

7. I seem to dislike events or moments where I feel:

_____

_____

8. Therefore, feeling _____ seems to be important to my happiness.

9. As a child, I wanted to be the following when I grew up:

A. _____

B. _____

C. _____

D. _____

E. _____

How have my interests changed since then? How are they the same? How does my current occupation relate to these interests?

_____

_____

_____

10. Things that I can do that most other people cannot do:

    A. _____

    B. _____

    C. _____

    D. _____

    E. _____

11. Things other people seem to be able to do better than I can:

    A. _____

    B. _____

    C. _____

    D. _____

    E. _____

12. Which of the skills I just listed do I want to improve? What can I do in the next year to begin to improve those skills?

    _____

    _____

13. I feel that in my life so far I have missed out on:

    _____

    _____

14. I think it is still possible for me to pursue the following things:

    A. _____

    B. _____

    C. _____

    D. _____

    E. _____

15. I think that it is no longer possible for me to pursue the following things:

    A. _____

    B. _____

(continued)

C. _____

D. _____

E. _____

16. In *one* year:

A. I want my job to be _____.

B. I want my family to be _____.

C. I want to see myself as a(n) _____ in the world.

17. In *five* years:

A. I want my job to be _____.

B. I want my family to be _____.

C. I want to see myself as a(n) _____

in the world.

18. *Today,* I can do the following thing(s) in the direction of those goals:

_____

_____

19. *This week,* I can do the following thing(s) in the direction of those goals:

_____

_____

20. *This month,* I can do the following thing(s) in the direction of those goals:

_____

_____

21. *This year,* I can do the following thing(s) in the direction of those goals:

_____

_____

3

Seek Opportunity

*Luck to me is something else: hard work—and
realizing what is opportunity and what isn't.*

—LUCILLE BALL

PUT YOURSELF IN LUCK'S WAY

*O*nce when Napoleon was asked to promote
one of his officers to a general's rank, he listened patiently to the
recital of the officer's accomplishments, the battles he'd participated in, his tactical skills—all those qualities traditionally considered to be essential in a general. Then he asked a single
question: "But is he lucky?"

He didn't mean does this man win money at the gambling
casino or have a tendency to find four-leaf clovers. He meant: Is
this a man who creates his own opportunities and seizes fortune
when it presents itself to him? Does he *make* his own luck?

There's a saying when somebody does something risky and
dangerous: We say they put themselves "in harm's way." I'd like to
propose an equivalent saying for people who seek out opportunity and create their own luck: *They put themselves in luck's way.*

If you're just sitting at home wishing you were more successful, trust me, opportunity will not knock. Seeking success and
happiness is an active process. You have to make yourself avail-

able to opportunity, put yourself in situations where opportunities will arise. There's another saying: "Luck is when opportunity meets preparation."

Success isn't an accident. It's the result of a process that can be learned. And a huge element of success—of "luck"—is preparation.

Think of the brilliant athletes we love to watch as they play in the Super Bowl or compete in the Olympics. It's not just "luck" that got them there, and it's no accident that they play so magnificently. They've been preparing all their lives for that moment. They train eight hours or more each and every day. They regulate their diet and their living habits. Their awesome performances are the culmination of a lifetime of hard work. They didn't sit around the house watching reruns and wishing that an NFL talent scout would come knocking on the door.

When you've identified what you think is your goal and your path, then you owe it to yourself to give it your very best shot. That means doing the research and preparation required, whatever that may be. You can't just say you want to find Mr. Right, then sit back and wait for him to knock on your door. The only man you're going to meet that way is the pizza-delivery guy. You need to find out where are the opportunities for you to meet Mr. Right, then avail yourself of them.

Remember the single mother in chapter 2, struggling just to pay the rent and feed her child, who had the dream of someday becoming a filmmaker? Rather than give in to despair and just sit at home wondering where the rent money was going to come from, she devoted a part of her energies and time each week to developing the best possible portfolio of her photography, which she could then show to agencies that might help her take the next step in her career. Simply by putting herself out there in the world, announcing her presence to the industry, she was putting herself in luck's way. Who knows what opportunity might arise from a chance meeting in some agent's office, or at the studio where she rented darkroom time and was in contact with other photographers?

As I was in the early stages of developing StarMedia and again with VOY, I spent a tremendous amount of time pitching my vision to strangers who were in a position somehow to help me realize my goal: potential investors in StarMedia, Hollywood studios that might produce television shows for VOY, and so on. And I was always amazed at how simply meeting people almost invariably results in new opportunities.

Often such opportunities—such luck—came from meetings I'd gone to with low expectations. In the early days of StarMedia, I once tried to arrange a meeting with the CEO of a company. He was unavailable, and I ended up sitting across a conference table from an executive who was in middle management and whose job wasn't particularly relevant to what I'd come to discuss. As the meeting progressed, he suddenly revealed that he'd been in the Peace Corps in Latin America and loved it, and was excited about what I was trying to do there. He didn't think his boss would get behind the project, but he suggested a list of other people I should contact—people I wouldn't have known about otherwise. And a few of them turned out to be quite helpful.

Opportunities come to you like that if you put yourself out there where you can bump into them. It may seem like random chance, but it really isn't. I had actively put myself in a situation, possibly wasting my time with this low-level manager, but it paid off.

That happens all the time—if you actively seek fortune and take the risks. You're much more likely to luck into your soul mate if you're going to the church socials, taking tango lessons, signing up for the online dating service, and so on.

There's another element of chance that's important to know:

The shortest path to your goal isn't always a straight line. For our thirty-year-old wanna-be dancer from chapter 2, going to an audition at her nearest ballet company is almost surely not going to land her a place in the *corps de ballet*. She's going to be up against a bunch of well-trained sixteen-year-olds. She will most likely never become a prima ballerina, and auditioning is only going to make her look like a delusional oddity to the people running the ballet company.

But maybe she should get that job or internship in the office of the dance company. Get to know the people and let them get to know her. Learn the world of professional dance. Take a variety of dance classes. Be part—not just a desirous observer—of the dance world. Who knows what opportunity might come from that, how they might invite her to participate? She may never be a ballet star, but she might get to participate meaningfully and happily in the world of dance.

ALLOW YOURSELF TO WANDER

Not all those that wander are lost.

—J. R. R. TOLKIEN

I know a woman who is a gifted massage therapist. Sally brings healing and peace of mind to her clients on a daily basis. Unfortunately, it doesn't bring *her* much happiness. It's not a calling, not a vocation—it's just a skill she learned, and it's become a dull routine. She feels stuck, bored, just drifting through her life.

When I asked her what it is that she truly wants to do with her life, her answer was disturbing: "I don't know. I've never really thought about it. In fact, I don't even know what I don't know."

Sadly, many people find themselves in her situation. They may own a framing shop, be raising four kids, and have an SUV and a snowmobile in the garage, but it all adds up to "a so-called life." They not only are not fulfilled in their current lives, they can't even look inside themselves and identify something that might fulfill them. They can't choose a goal, let alone map out a path toward it.

While I believe that everyone should have a plan, and should be moving every day toward their goals, it's also important to be flexible about the path your life takes. You need to leave space for exploration and experimentation as well. This is especially true if, like that massage therapist, you can't determine what it is you should be doing with your life—or, like our forty-five-year-old wanna-be pitcher, you're somehow stuck in old dreams and don't know what else to do with yourself. There can be an enormous utility to simply looking around at the world and thinking, "What else is there I might try?"—things you've never done before, or maybe were scared to try. **Give yourself permission to experiment with new experiences that may bring new focus or new joy to your life.**

If we agree that life is about the journey, not the destination, then you owe it to yourself to make the journey as interesting and varied as possible. I did not go to Nepal with the intention of having a vision that would change my life. My motive was much simpler—I went because Nepal seemed the most different and exotic environment in which I could put myself and my wife. There was no other logic to choosing Nepal; it wasn't my lifelong dream destination or anything like that. We picked it literally because it was very far away from our daily lives and seemed like it would be a very different and even alien environment.

And it certainly was. Everything about India and Nepal was new to us. Placing yourself in a setting that's foreign to you has a way of putting your own world in perspective. When you expose yourself to ways other people live and think, their radically different worldview, it can't help but make you reflect on your own life. That trip to India and Nepal brought me to a revelation that changed my life and, frankly, changed Latin America.

The lesson I've taken from that experience is not to overplan my life. To allow for an element of chance and make room in my life for opportunities to discover new ideas, new people, new experiences that may give me new insights into myself and help me fine-tune my plans.

Just as you don't have to go to Nepal to find your own mountaintop, you don't have to travel to foreign lands to encounter new ideas and experiences. The world is full of activities you haven't tried, knowledge you haven't acquired, skills you never developed, people you've never met. What we "know" is a tiny subset of what is knowable.

If you never learned how to swim or ride a bike or dance the mambo, maybe now's the time. If you're the sedentary type, maybe you want to try something physically adventurous, like skydiving, rock climbing, or tae kwon do lessons. Take up fencing or ballroom dancing or white-water rafting. You may like it. You may hate it. You'll certainly develop a feeling of accomplishment just for being brave enough to try it. You may meet interesting people whose own areas of knowledge and experience may lead your life in various new and positive directions.

Adventures of the mind are just as exciting, and are very easy to come by. For instance, I love to read history, and if I let myself all I'd ever read is history books. So periodically I'll make myself stop reading history for a while. The next five books I read will be ones I normally wouldn't read, on topics I know nothing about—black holes in space, the lives and customs of Gypsies in Romania, the structure of the human genome, whatever. I have exposed myself to all sorts of new ideas and knowledge that way.

You can sign up for classes at a nearby college, craft center, or adult-learning center. Take a course in astronomy or cooking or Italian or pottery. Pick a subject or skill you always wanted to know more about, or just choose one at random. Some topics will no doubt turn out to be dead ends for you—but at least now you'll know you have no interest in or aptitude for that subject.

But who knows what latent talents or hidden interests you'll discover? Who knows where that new knowledge and experience will lead you? Maybe some people in your Italian class will plan a group trip to Tuscany, where you'll discover an appreciation for Renaissance frescoes that opens entirely new avenues in your life.

Opening yourself up to new experiences has a number of benefits. On the simplest level, it's an antidote to the sort of boredom and apathy that massage therapist was exhibiting. *Boredom and apathy are enemies of a happy life.* They're a self-reinforcing vicious cycle: The more bored and apathetic you feel, the less inclined you are even to try to change your situation. Allowing yourself to experience something new breaks the boredom habit and gives you renewed interest in life.

On another level, trying new experiences and finding you like them can help you overcome the phobias and fears that inhibit people from living their lives fully—fear of the unknown, fear of failure, fear of embarrassment. Think of the times in your life when you faced down a fear—when you were a kid and learned to swim or high-dive or ride a bike without training wheels—and what a thrilling sense of freedom and empowerment came from conquering that fear. Remember how learning to ride that bike unlocked a whole new world of opportunities for you.

There's a wonderful scene in the comic movie *What About Bob?* Bob is a neurotic paranoid whose laundry list of phobias prevents him from living anything remotely like a full or happy life. When Bob's psychiatrist goes away on vacation, Bob is so terrified of abandonment that he horns in on the analyst's lakeside resort, where he proceeds literally to drive the shrink crazy with his aggressive neediness. But Bob's presence, annoying as he is, also presents learning opportunities for the psychiatrist's family. Bob is terrified of drowning; the analyst's adolescent son is drawn to the water but is afraid to dive in. While trying to show Bob that there's nothing to fear about the water, the boy unconsciously overcomes his own concerns and dives in. The unplanned en-counter with Bob opens him to new experience and enriches his life. (We'll return to the "fear factor" later.)

The learning experiences shouldn't end just because you be-came an adult. **Your entire life can and should be a learning ex-perience and an adventure.** No human being is complete and perfect. We're all works-in-progress. You may well surprise your-self with talents you never knew you had or areas of knowledge you never explored.

Especially if you're really not sure what you want out of life and what you want to do with your life, opening yourself to ran-dom experiences may well help you discover a positive direction and a path. It's okay to "wander" from one experience to another this way, because you never know where that wandering may lead you to. There's an enormous difference between wandering and merely drifting aimlessly through life. Drifting is passive and leads nowhere; wandering is active and always leads you somewhere. Over time, putting those new experiences in the context of who you are will start pointing you in certain life directions. You'll get a better handle on what gives you pleasure and what doesn't, what feels natural to you and what doesn't.

Get active. Discover. Experience. Learn. Shake up your world. Challenge yourself to grow and try new things.

REAL VERSUS FALSE OPPORTUNITY

And now for a cautionary note.

Unfortunately, it's not always easy to distinguish between what's a real opportunity—an unexpected chance to get closer to your goal—and what's merely a very attractive distraction or di-version from your goal. It requires constant analysis. So many chance opportunities pop up in your path that at first blush seem either absolutely positive or completely negative—some things that, at first glance, you think you would never do, and other things that you just want to jump right on. **If you have a strategic goal for your life and you keep focused on how to achieve it, then you can analyze each opportunity as it arises and make an informed decision about it.** Will this truly bring me closer to my happiness and success? Or is this something that looks really fun and "cool" now but will ultimately lead me astray from my path and farther from my true goal?

Consider that couple in chapter 2 who suddenly found themselves with the chance to have their own restaurant. It's easy to understand their initial emotional response. Here was something they'd often dreamed about, something that looked like it would be so much fun to do. Let's go for it!

But was it really an opportunity that would move them closer to their life's goal, or more in the nature of an irresistible side-trip? There's a difference between your life's dream and mere daydreams. I've always daydreamed, say, that someday I'd like to pilot a Learjet. But it's only a daydream, not something that's at the core of my being. If the opportunity comes along and it doesn't distract me too much from pursuing my true goals, then hey, I'll do it. But you can't open and operate a restaurant on a lark. It's very hard work. It required the total commitment of both partners' lives.

I doubt if they spent much time analyzing this apparent opportunity before they jumped. And that is a critical step. There's a list of questions I'd have wanted them to answer before they took the plunge. Why do we think we'd be good restaurateurs? What is this business about? Who are our competitors? Who are our consumers? Why aren't there other upscale restaurants in this neighborhood?

If you can answer all those questions and you truly believe you're destined to own a restaurant, then you owe it to yourself to be as successful as possible. You owe it yourself to develop a deep understanding of the business and become as knowledgeable as you can about the objective conditions to being successful. Otherwise you're just betting on the lottery.

In the introduction I described several junctures in my life where I was presented with opportunities that I had to think very carefully about. And in one instance, at least, I learned the hard way how not to jump at false opportunity. When I was a young executive at AT&T, you'll recall, I looked to the future and saw myself rocketing up the corporate ladder there. I was sure that this was my goal, that it was what would make me happy. So I worked like a madman to make that happen, and I succeeded. But when I got the big promotion I'd thought I wanted, I suddenly realized that it would not make me happy at all. My need to create and innovate would be stifled in that position. Clearly, I hadn't thought it all through correctly when I set out to achieve that goal.

The odd thing is, I'd already been presented with another false opportunity, which I'd correctly analyzed and rejected. Before I went to work for AT&T, there was a position Ogilvy & Mather had offered me in New Zealand. It was an extremely tempting offer. It was a great job for a twenty-five-year-old—I would be the managing director of Ogilvy & Mather's Wellington office. My wife and I were young and ready for a travel adventure. But when I analyzed that opportunity relative to my long-term goals, it seemed likely that a move to New Zealand might be fun but it would be a side step on my path, nothing more. So we turned it down—and I went to work for AT&T.

If you keep focused on your ultimate goal, it helps you make tactical decisions like that. This is a daily occurrence for me. Everything that comes my way I consider from the perspective of "Does this fit my strategic plan or not?" That doesn't mean I have every link in the chain already figured out. Absolutely not—

I have some steps planned, but there are plenty of gaps between this step and the next. There's only so much of the future you can micromanage from the present. Random occurrences you could not possibly have foreseen or prepared for are part of everyone's life. Maybe this new, completely unexpected opportunity that comes down the pike today is one of the links. Maybe it's not. Analyze it, try to see if it fits or not, and make your decision accordingly.

REVIEW

- Success isn't an accident. It's the result of an active process of planning, preparation, and seeking opportunity.

- The shortest path to your goal isn't always a straight line. Give yourself permission to experiment with new experiences that may bring new focus or new joy to your life.

- Your entire life can and should be a learning experience and an adventure. Get active. Discover. Experience. Learn. Shake up your world. Challenge yourself to grow and try new things.

- If you have a strategic goal for your life and you keep focused on how to achieve it, then you can analyze each opportunity as it arises and make an informed decision about it.

EXERCISE: Drawing a Road Map

There were no road maps of the United States when Dr. Horatio Jackson set out on the first cross-country automobile trip, in 1903. Similarly, when you have identified a strategic goal for yourself, you have to draw your own road map to get you there. You envision a future you want to create, then think through the incremental steps you can take to get there. In reality, your journey may take unpredictable twists and turns, and you will need to be flexible enough to take advantage of unexpected opportunities when they present themselves. But without a road map as a guide, you will find yourself wandering in the wilderness.

In this exercise, you literally draw yourself a map: "This is where I want to go, and these are the steps." To start, you may want to choose a goal that's not too distant—maybe six months or a year from now.

1. Identify your goal and write it down on a clean sheet of paper.

2. Identify the skills you will need to acquire and actions you will need to take to accomplish that goal. Write them down.

3. Identify people you need to inspire and enlist to join you on this quest. Write down their names.

4. Now flip the paper over. Draw a symbol for your goal at the right side of the page. Draw a line across the page from this symbol to the left side of the page. This is your path.

5. Now draw symbols for the skills, actions, and people you identified in steps 2 and 3. Place them along the path in the order you think they should go.

   You've just drawn yourself a basic road map.
   Fxample:
   In six months I want to have a driver's license. To get there, I have to get my parents' permission and assistance, apply to the Motor Vehicle Department for a learner's permit, get my mom to teach me how to drive, and finally, pass the driver's test.

(continued)

I write these down on a sheet of paper. I flip it over, then draw a car on the right side of the page, and a line from there to the left side. From left to right along this line, I draw two faces (my parents), a key (the learner's permit), my mom's face (teaching me to drive), and a diploma (passing the test).

This is my map to a driver's license. As I progress through the six months, I can refer to it to see how far along the path I am, and what's left to do.

That's a simple example, but it demonstrates how the process works. The more distant your goal is, and the more steps you need to take to get there, the more you will find this mapping technique helps both to line those steps up in the best sequence and to monitor your progress.

Deconstruct the Future

The best way to predict the future is to invent it.

— ALAN C. KAY, Apple

*I*n sports, there are long-distance runners who impress the rest of us with their capacity to run a marathon, which is 26.2 miles long. But then there's a small, almost "underground" set of athletes who are called "ultra-endurance runners." They've stretched their running way beyond 26.2 miles. They'll run fifty or a hundred miles in a single race. Not in stages or relays—they just keep running, without sleep, until they reach the finish line. A typical marathon takes about three hours to run; a hundred-mile race takes twenty-four hours or more of virtually nonstop physical exertion. It may well be the most grueling sport on earth.

When asked how he can possibly run that far, Dean Karnazes, one of the greatest of these athletes, has a very instructive answer. He says he runs the first fifty miles with his legs and the last fifty miles with his mind. He visualizes crossing the finish line, then mentally breaks down the race into smaller increments. He focuses on making the next five miles or making it to the top of the next hill, and when that's done, he focuses on the next stage, and the next. But all the while, he holds that image of the finish line steady in his mind, like a beacon pulling him forward.

What Karnazes is doing is an extremely powerful mental exercise. **He envisions a future in which he is achieving a seemingly far-off goal. Then he deconstructs that future into smaller tactical steps that will lead him to that goal.**

You may have seen the PBS documentary *Horatio's Drive*, or read the book by the same name. It describes the adventure of Dr. Horatio Nelson Jackson, who made the first cross-country automobile trip in America in 1903. It's a rollicking tale. On a dare, Jackson bet a man $50 that he could drive from San Francisco to New York City in under ninety days.

To understand what an outrageous vision that was, you have to know that in 1903 there were only 150 miles of paved roads in the continental United States, and they were mostly in cities. The vast continent was crossed mostly by dirt roads over which no automobile had ever traveled. There were no gas stations, no road maps. Jackson's car had only two gears—forward and reverse—no windshield or roof, and a top speed of thirty miles per hour. As one reviewer of the book put it, Jackson's dream of driving cross-country "appeared about as feasible as a moon shot."

But like all successful people, Jackson was able to hold a vision of rolling that car into Manhattan firmly in his mind, and proceeded to complete his journey in small stages, advancing a little bit every day. He did this despite incredible hardships, many forced side-trips and diversions, and almost daily obstacles—rocky roads that routinely punctured his tires; slippery, barely controlled descents down deadly precipices in the Rockies; vast fields of mud that threatened to suck the car under; and frequent breakdowns.

Jackson entered New York City sixty-three days after he started out, collected his $50, and was hailed as a national hero. More important, his accomplishment inspired Americans to dream for the first time of a national system of paved roads that would allow everyone to drive from coast to coast and to all points in between. In no small way, our interstate highway system was inspired by this visionary and his "crazy" dream. By envisioning and accomplishing the "impossible," he transformed the United States.

The idea of deconstructing the future is a premise I first encountered when reading Homer's *Iliad* and *Odyssey*. In Homer's epic poems, there are basically two kinds of creatures, humans and gods. Humans live in linear time: They get up and brush their teeth and go through their day. The gods live in horizontal time: They look down on the plane of human existence from on top of Mount Olympus, and they can see all of time—past, present, and future—at once, laid out below them like a chessboard. As the humans move through time like chess pieces, the gods are able to observe not just what's happening now but what happened before and what will happen in the future.

Unlike Homer's gods, **no one can actually see the future. The future doesn't exist. The point is not** *seeing* **the future. The point is** *making* **the future.** It is projecting your will into some future time to create some series of events that together can lead to a vision—that is what I did to create StarMedia. Then you can map out the component events that lead up to that future. You, as an agent in the world and as part of the future-making machine, can be the author of your own fate. You can visualize what a possible future would look like, and then say, "Okay, to get to that point—five steps ahead, twenty, thirty steps ahead—what are some of the things that must occur for that future to become real?"

Because there's no preset future, I'm free to allow my mind to roam through many possible futures. I can see myself winning the Boston Marathon, becoming the king of Spain, or creating a new entrepreneurial venture.

Now I start sifting through those futures. King of Spain is never going to happen, because I wasn't born into the royal family, so I can set that one aside as pure fantasy. I suppose I *could* become a Learjet pilot or win the New York Marathon, but since they're not germane to my true goals, I can't see myself devoting the time and effort either would require. Creative entrepreneurship, however, is precisely what I want and need to do with my life right now.

Now I begin to deconstruct that future. What are the steps I can take that will get me there? What are the tactical maneuvers? What talents do I need to bring to bear? What skills am I lacking that I need to develop? Whom do I need to inspire and enlist to join me on this quest?

This is not a one-time-only, cut-and-dried exercise, for the simple reason that the context keeps changing over time. Just as you are creating the future, so is everyone else. The world will not stand still while you're making your plans. If you're planning for a future that's only a year off—say, you see yourself getting promoted to regional marketing manager in charge of all East Coast accounts—the context may not shift dramatically. You can fairly easily map out steps that can lead you to that goal. But if your plan, like Laurie's in chapter 2, is to be a filmmaker five or ten years from now, you have to be open to the changes that will occur over that time. This is why I stress flexibility. When you're deconstructing a future that's five or ten years down the road, openness to chance and the ability to see and grasp an unplanned opportunity become critical.

Knowing that you are the author of your future is intensely powerful. Suddenly, all the barriers that are in front of you melt away when you know that there's no predetermined future, only the one you create.

When I founded StarMedia, and we were maxing out credit

cards and had a staff of only four or five, there was never any ambiguity about where we were going. I knew *exactly* where we were going. We were going to become a major media company. And everything we did on a day-to-day basis—sometimes annoying, sometimes difficult as it was—all of those tasks and challenges were eminently manageable because they were just details in a much bigger picture.

As political scientist John Schaar writes, "The future is not some place we are going, but one we are creating. The paths to it are not found but made, and the activity of making them changes both the maker and the destination."

DON'T FEAR MISTAKES — LEARN FROM THEM

Do I always make the right decision? Of course not. I'm human. Everyone knows this. Still, *fear of failure* is one of the worst inhibitors in the human psyche. Some people fear making a mistake so much that it paralyzes them into complete inactivity. They think they'd rather do nothing at all than do something "wrong." Sometimes, our fear of making a mistake is what causes us to make a mistake. In sports, "choking" is a well-known phenomenon. We've all seen the brilliant golfer who blows a tournament on the last three holes because he let his fear of losing ruin his concentration and his game. The kicker who's brought into the football game in the last ten seconds to try for the winning field goal is well aware that if he can't keep his mind free from fear of failure he'll never be loose and focused enough to give it his best shot.

Probably no one fears mistakes more than those in the medical and health professions. One tiny wrong move of a surgeon's scalpel may kill the patient. A single missed diagnosis, or prescribing the wrong medicine, can have catastrophic results. And

What would life be if we had no courage to attempt anything?
—VINCENT VAN GOGH

yet, especially in the development of new medicines, mistakes and accidents have sometimes led to discoveries that changed the course of history. Insulin, penicillin, quinine, the smallpox vaccine, and X-rays were all discovered by accident. (By the way, laughing gas, dynamite, Velcro, Teflon, Post-its, and even cornflakes were also the results of mistakes or accidents.)

We all make mistakes. Curiously, we tend to be more forgiving of other people's fallibility than our own. We'll tell a friend, "Hey, it's all right. Everyone makes mistakes. Don't be so hard on yourself." Then, when *we* make a mistake, we kick ourselves and agonize over it. "How could I have been so *stupid*? I am a complete idiot." We forget that other people are as willing as we are to overlook mistakes.

As you pursue your goals, you are surely going to make mistakes, errors of judgment, missteps. So how do you survive a mistake? How do you recoup when you go for something, start doing it, and realize, "Oh man, this was a mistake"?

None of us has the omniscience of the gods. Unless you're holed up in a room somewhere refusing to have any engagement with the world, a tragedy in itself, you're going to make mistakes. Creative endeavor is especially fraught with mistakes and missteps. The best-loved novels in the world were revised and revised before anyone ever read them. The greatest painters make mistakes and paint over them. If you structure your life so as never to make any mistakes, you will almost certainly not have the courage and the intuitive freedom to take risks and maximize opportunities when they arise. You'll be so afraid of making mistakes that you'll never commit yourself to your success.

I've made many errors. My first reaction, naturally, is to kick myself about it, to tell myself I can't make any more mistakes. Which is, of course, unrealistic. No one is perfect. And no mistake is deadly except the one that kills you.

The first thing you have to do is not take it personally. Making a mistake does not mean that you're somehow an unworthy human being. **Mistakes aren't character flaws.** They're a natural result of being an active person, engaged in the world of human endeavor. I try to remember this, and stop kicking myself for whatever error I commit.

Then I try to see what I can learn from my mistake. I analyze it, the way I analyze everything I do. What was wrong about what I did? How did I choose to do that? What pattern in my thinking or emotions was I following when I made this mistake? Have I made this same kind of mistake before? If so, how can I be aware of this tendency in myself and be on guard against it?

Your mistakes can often teach you more than your successes. Buckminster Fuller, one of the most innovative architects and inventors of the twentieth century, wrote, "Whatever humans have learned had to be learned as a consequence only of trial and error experience. Humans have learned only through mistakes." The meetings I have today in Hollywood are very different from the meetings I had a year ago. There are codes of behavior there, certain expectations, certain systems and processes that you need to be aware of. I've learned a lot about how Hollywood works that I didn't know a year ago, and adjusted my plans and expectations accordingly.

And finally, the most important step: **Forgive yourself.** Okay, you made a mistake. It only proves that you're a human being.

Success is the ability to go from one failure to another with no loss of enthusiasm.

—WINSTON CHURCHILL

HEROES

While each of us must choose our own goals and our own path through life, that doesn't mean we can't learn from the experiences and the examples of others. We can all use role models.

I truly believe **everyone needs a hero.** And I mean a hero who's almost supernatural. Not in the sense of a divine being, but someone who identified a goal that was almost unimaginable, envisioned a future that no one else could see, and overcame whatever was thrown in his or her way.

Why? Because in the moment of creation, in that lonely moment when it's just you and your idea, and all you're hearing is negative feedback from other people—in that moment when all rational thinking is telling you this is a questionable idea, yet the irrational, passionate belief inside you is telling you this can happen, this is a great idea and only I can achieve it—at that moment you cannot be alone. In that moment you have to be able to draw on someone who can inspire you. And it needs to be someone almost supernatural, because what they have achieved is so much greater than what you need to get done today, or tomorrow, that it makes your mountain look that much smaller and easier to climb in comparison.

For me, that hero has been Sir Winston Churchill. I suppose that's a weird choice for a young Latin living in the United States. But he works for me, and let me explain why.

Churchill was born in 1874 into the heart of British power and influence, the son of a prominent politician, Lord Randolph Churchill, himself the son of the Duke of Marlborough. But his path through life was anything but easy, and he achieved his own personal Grail—his "walk with destiny," as he interestingly put it—only very late in life, when, as prime minister, he led Britain to victory against the Nazis in World War II.

As a human being, he was far from perfect. Throughout his life he was prone to fits of self-doubt and deep depression. In political and social terms he was an archconservative. He absolutely did not understand how the world was changing in the twentieth century, and he still believed in an idealized nineteenth-century world of the British Empire, regardless of the horrible impact that empire had on millions of people's lives—in places like India, for example.

Churchill tried his hand at many things before reaching his ultimate goal in life. In his young manhood, he proved himself to be a fearless military officer and saw action in many battles. He was also a fine writer of both history and journalism, for which he would win, late in life, a Nobel Prize. He became a member of Parliament in his mid-twenties, held various government positions throughout his life, and, despite a lifelong speech impediment, distinguished himself as one of the greatest political speakers of the twentieth century. But none of this fulfilled for him his sense of his own destiny.

Then the Nazis plunged Europe into World War II. By 1940, they had overrun all of Europe and had just defeated France. France at that time had seemingly amassed the most powerful army in Europe and was considered the ultimate bulwark against Nazi expansion. The German onslaught simply crushed it (a tragic and definitive rebuttal of the French doctrine of static defense). In the process of Germany's overrunning France, Britain (France's ally) lost all of its military equipment, all of its supplies—every tank, truck, gun—and the remains of the British army were pushed back to the sea, to Dunkirk, where they made a desperate last-minute escape.

Winston Churchill became prime minister in 1940. He was in his mid-sixties. Looking across the English Channel, he saw hundreds of thousands of German soldiers, and all the might of the German Luftwaffe, poised to invade. Britain had virtually no army left. Unlike France, it was a small, defenseless island nation. The Germans should have had no trouble defeating it.

Yet Winston Churchill, speaking before Parliament, told Britain, and the world, that his objective was total victory over the Germans. He said that in spite of the obvious odds, in spite of the oncoming terror, Britain would triumph over evil. He told the British people, "I have nothing to offer but blood, toil, tears, and sweat"—but promised them that the result in the end would be victory.

And then he did something that appeared absolutely insane. The British air force had been reduced to a seemingly inadequate number of planes. The German Luftwaffe greatly outnumbered them. The "logical" thing to do under these circumstances would be to conserve those planes to defend the skies over Britain, to defend the homeland from German invasion. Instead, Churchill hurled those few remaining planes at Germany. They bombed German cities and war factories. Instead of cowering in a defensive mode, knowing that in a few weeks they were going to be taken over and turned into Nazi slaves, the British went on the attack.

The psychological impact of this brave, daring act was so powerful in people's minds—in Germany, and in Britain and among her allies—that it became one of the turning points of the war. Psychologically, Germany lost the momentum at this moment and never regained it. If Britain had risked an offensive, the Germans thought, clearly she had the strength to stop an invasion. So the Germans held off their Channel crossing. It would take five more long and bloody years to defeat them, but this apparently insane, illogical act put Britain on a path to victory.

"Every day you may make progress," Churchill wrote. "Every step may be fruitful. Yet there will stretch out before you an ever-lengthening, ever-ascending, ever-improving path. You know you will never get to the end of the journey. But this, so far from discouraging, only adds to the joy and glory of the climb."

When you're starting out on your own path toward your own personal goals, to have a figure like that—who was faced with life-and-death decisions for his entire country and indeed the

Western world, and who fought to create the circumstances for success at the bleakest possible moment—can make your own trials and obstacles look a lot smaller and more manageable.

History is full of heroes, many of them great military, political, or spiritual leaders whom you can emulate in your own life: Gandhi, Alexander, Churchill, Marie Curie, Simón Bolívar, Franklin Roosevelt, Martin Luther King, Jr., Mother Teresa—to name just a few. None of them was perfect, and some of them, like Churchill and Alexander, were in fact deeply flawed individuals. That's all the more reason why they can be useful to us as models: They overcame their limitations, met their challenges, and achieved their goals, often against seemingly outrageous odds. If they could do it, why can't you?

REVIEW

- The successful person envisions a future in which he is achieving a seemingly far-off goal. Then he deconstructs that future into smaller tactical steps that will lead him to that goal.

- No one can actually see the future. The future doesn't exist. The point is not *seeing* the future. The point is *making* the future.

- Don't fear mistakes. Mistakes aren't character flaws. Life is a learning process. Your mistakes can often teach you more than your successes.

- Everyone needs a hero.

EXERCISE: Who Are My Heroes?

We should all have heroes and role models—people we admire and whose character or actions we try to emulate. When we're young and impressionable, we become infatuated with all sorts of figures who appeal to us for various reasons. They may include fictional superheroes, pop stars, sports figures, a great teacher; they may also include those we admire for the wrong reasons, like the "bad" older kid we think is "cool" when we're going through a rebellious phase. As we grow and mature, what we value and admire in others tends to change; ideally, we become wiser about looking for positive qualities in others that we seek to develop in ourselves.

Try this simple exercise to see how your heroes have changed over time—and what that can tell you about yourself and your values.

1. When I was a *child,* my heroes and/or the people I most looked up to were:
    A. _____
    B. _____
    C. _____
    D. _____
    E. _____

2. When I was a *teenager,* my heroes and/or the people I most looked up to were:
    A. _____
    B. _____
    C. _____
    D. _____
    E. _____

3. *Today,* my heroes and/or the people I most look up to are:
    A. _____
    B. _____
    C. _____

(continued)

D. _____

E. _____

4. How have my heroes and role models changed since I was a child? How are they the same? What, if anything, do they have in common? What do I admire most about them? What does this tell me about the qualities and characteristics I'd most like to develop in myself?

_____

_____

_____

_____

_____

_____

_____

_____

_____

_____

Assert Your Vision

First they ignore you, then they laugh at you, then they fight you, then you win.

— MAHATMA GANDHI

WHAT IS REALITY?

*T*hroughout the history of mankind, great minds of every civilization—philosophers, scientists, theologians, mystics—have struggled to answer this deceptively simple question. The very fact that they've come up with so many conflicting answers should tell you something.

Eastern philosophies and religions have tended to say that the world we think we know through our five senses and through logic and reason is all an illusion or a dream. (I remember the first time someone put this sort of idea into my head as a kid. "How do you know that this all isn't a dream, and we're all not just characters in that dream?" It had a profound effect on me. It was the beginning of my understanding that I could actively shape my life and the world around me.) Therefore, reality cannot be grasped through logic and science, but only through intuition.

Until quite recently, Western thinkers took a "harder" view. Reality was what we could perceive through our senses. It could be measured and mapped and explained through logic and reason, mathematics and the sciences. The universe was orderly and rational and conformed to rigid laws.

One problem with this view was that what we thought we knew about reality was always limited by our senses and by the current state of our mathematical models and scientific know-how. For thousands of years people "knew" the Earth was flat because they could see it with their own eyes; they "knew" the sun revolved around the Earth because they saw it rise and set every day. People were so confident that these things were true that when courageous minds like Galileo, Copernicus, and Columbus demonstrated otherwise, many were punished or even put to death for their effrontery. (To this day, right here in the U.S.A., a handful of people still refuse to believe that the Earth is round. They even have their own organization, the Flat Earth Society.)

Our logic and senses tell us that a table is solid. We know that if we put a coffee cup down it won't fall through to the floor. But we also all know from school that in fact that table—and the cup and the floor, for that matter—are actually arrangements of numerous tiny, whirring atomic particles. The cup can't pass through the table because of the attracting forces holding those particles in very close relation to one another. It's a whole different definition of "solid" than that which refers to what we can see and feel.

Our senses perceive the space in which we all move around in three dimensions: length, width, and height. For many centuries, Western scientists used the mathematics of algebra and geometry to map and describe this three-dimensional universe. Then Sir Isaac Newton realized that to understand the universe more fully, we also needed to be able to describe how things move through this three-dimensional space and through time (the fourth dimension). He created a whole new branch of mathematics, calculus, to do that.

In the twentieth century, physicists began to question seriously just how much of "reality" can be observed and measured. The more they learned about "reality" on the subatomic level, the more inconsistencies they found with "reality" on the everyday, macroscopic level. For example, subatomic particles, contrary to everything we think we know about "reality," seem to be able to exist in two (or more) places at once.

Today, theoretical physicists have pushed way beyond Newton's four-dimensional model of reality. According to the modern physics of string theory, which theorizes that all those tiny whirring particles are like minute beads arranged on vibrating "strings" of energy, there may be as many as twenty-six dimensions. There also may be not just the one universe we inhabit but an infinite number of "parallel" universes. Another theoretical wing of advanced physics argues that the universe may be like a giant hologram—in a sense, an illusion.

In short, the gap between Eastern philosophy and Western science is a lot smaller today than it used to be.

Put in terms of your own life, the message of all this is profound and liberating. **There is no single objective truth. There is only this subjective reality—a reality you can envision and then make real**. Your goals are not limited by anyone else's definition of reality. You can choose your own future. You can be author of your own success. Knowing that reality is subjective frees you to roam in your imagination through many possible futures.

I have found that there are a lot of flat-earthers in the business world. We celebrate entrepreneurs in our media, fiction, and movies, but the truth is the business community can be very short on vision, and the entrepreneur who succeeds often does so in spite of the accepted wisdom of the business world. For every great entrepreneurial vision that succeeds well enough to be celebrated, many more die because they were just so radical or innovative that they couldn't get the backing of the flat-earthers on Wall Street and in the corporate office.

When I was forming StarMedia, and again with VOY, I often ran into skeptics who were so wedded to their notions of "reality" that they could not even conceive of the vision I was presenting, let alone believe in it.

"But—but—but . . . you're trying to create a conglomerate out of nothing!" one potential VOY collaborator sputtered.

I smiled. "Yeah, so?"

"But—but—but that's *impossible*!"

"Why?" I asked.

I had another meeting with a man who started out telling me over and over that my ideas were "crazy." He actually used the word *crazy*. I patiently and calmly went on explaining my vision to him. By the end of the meeting, he was saying, "You know, this is just crazy enough that it might work!"

The simple truth is that the act of creation, in any field—whether you're creating paintings or novels or new business ventures—is inherently irrational. The idea that you can create something new out of nothing defies conventional belief. It's magical. In a sense, people still only believe in a "reality" they can see with their eyes and touch with their fingers. When asked how he could sculpt such divinely beautiful statues from big blocks of unformed marble, Michelangelo famously replied that the statue was always there, inside the rock—he just chipped away all the excess stone surrounding it. The creative person can look at that marble block and see the statue inside. But many people see only the rock. The successful person doesn't allow other people's lack of vision, their limited view of "reality," to hold him back.

THE POWER OF BELIEF

Although success takes many forms, there is a psychology that connects all successful people. When you look back across the

The thing always happens that you really believe in; and the belief in a thing makes it happen.

—FRANK LLOYD WRIGHT

four thousand or so years of written human history, a pattern emerges. Although each of us is unique, and we all must define and achieve success and happiness in our own individual ways, there seems to be a mind-set that, consciously or unconsciously, all successful people have exhibited. This is a mind-set we can all learn from and adapt for our own lives.

It may be the most critical psychological tool as you begin the process of self-actualization: **the power of belief.**

There are two kinds of belief that drive success. One is *reasoned belief*. You must have a black-and-white, fairly impeccable argument for what it is you want to create, what it is you want to do with your life, whether that's creating a new work of art, embarking upon your personal vocation, beginning an entrepreneurial venture—whatever it is. You must have a logical construct for it. You need to have done your homework and your preparation. This allows you to relate to the noncreative world. You're going to have to explain yourself to people who do not necessarily share your ideas and may not be very good at thinking creatively.

But reasoned belief is only half the game; you must also be driven by *passionate belief*. You must have that belief that your Grail is out there, that it is waiting for you to discover it, regardless of those people who tell you, "No, it's not." To create your unique vision, you must believe in yourself and your ability to recreate yourself.

I know this from my own life. When I set out to create Star-Media, I was acting out of a passionate belief in the power of this new thing called the Internet to transform the lives of all Latins across the world. By any objective standards, this was an irrational belief. It ran counter to the "realities" of Latin America. At that time, there were approximately fifty telephones for every one hundred inhabitants of the United States. In Brazil, there were only two. In Latin America, a computer cost the equivalent of the average person's entire annual salary. So it was totally "irrational" for me to say that the Internet was going to be a huge force for change in Latin America—unless you could see it, unless you believed it. And I did. And it worked. Today, there are about 50 million people in Latin America using the Internet. It's the fastest-growing region in the world for Internet use. I did that. That's the power of passionate belief.

If you look through history, every single successful person you find demonstrated that power. They projected their belief and their will out into the world, and made their dream a reality.

Mahatma Gandhi had the idea that he could lead the impoverished, disorganized people of India to throw off the dominion of the mighty British Empire—and that he could do it through nonviolent civil disobedience. What a thoroughly outlandish vision! But Gandhi believed in it with his whole being, and he never stopped believing in it through thirty years of failures and setbacks and disappointments. He was jailed, he was once nearly stoned to death by an angry mob, he was shot at and actually had bombs thrown at him, but he remained steadfast and unshakable in his belief. And in the end he liberated India.

Napoleon Bonaparte believed that one day he would rule France. He was born on the poor, ethnically Italian island of Corsica, physically and politically a very long distance from the halls of power in Paris. He was a short man; he spoke with an accent the Parisians found amusing; he was a lowly corporal in the French army. But he believed with his whole being that he was destined to lead France, and eventually he crowned himself its emperor.

As a young man, Bill Gates had a vision that one day virtually every household in the United States would have in it an appliance called a "personal computer." At the time, few people in business shared this vision. Computers belonged in research labs and corporate offices. Even if the average American family could afford one, what on earth would they do with it? Gates and his cohorts stuck with their belief, and as the founder of Microsoft he not only became the richest man in the world, but he also *transformed* the world with the PC.

The philosopher Hegel said that true heroes are those who envision a future, even if no one around them can, and then work toward making it happen for themselves and for everyone else. Because others have trouble seeing that future, it can be a lonely process. Eventually, when that future has become reality—when that future, in effect, has become the present—it will seem inevitable to everyone. Because it *has* happened, everyone now thinks it was always going to happen. It becomes "conventional wisdom"—after the fact.

DETERMINATION

Mythology is full of stories of heroes who go on perilous quests. They're beset by fantastic dangers, face grueling tests of courage, and encounter horrible evils, but their determination to complete their mission carries them through it all.

In Greek mythology, Jason was an infant when his father the king lost his throne to a usurper. Jason's mother spirited him away to the cave of a centaur, who raised him. When he reached manhood, Jason was determined to return to his kingdom and take back the throne. But as so often happens in Greek mythology, the gods on Olympus decided that he must first prove his worthiness by passing a number of tests and trials. He must go on a quest to capture the fabulous Golden Fleece.

Jason had a ship built, the magnificent Argo, and enlisted a crew of heroes, the Argonauts, who included Hercules. On their

The gem cannot be polished without friction, nor man perfected without trials.

—CHINESE PROVERB

voyage, they navigated the deadly passage through the clashing rocks Scylla and Charybdis; defeated monstrous creatures like the Harpies, who have women's heads on vulturelike bodies; tamed a team of giant, fire-breathing bulls; and, of course, dealt with the dragon who guarded the Fleece. Jason's determination (with some help from friendly gods) carried him through all of these trials. He captured the Fleece and was rewarded with success.

Greek myths are full of stories of heroes like Jason—and Hercules, Perseus, Odysseus, and Orpheus—who had to prove their determination over and over, passing numerous tests of strength, courage, and cunning, before the gods granted them success. The ancient Greeks intended these stories not only to entertain but to teach lessons for living. One of the lessons all the tales of heroes teach is **the power of relentless determination.**

In real life, successful people all exhibit the same relentless determination. Regardless of what gets in your way, regardless of any barrier, you must overcome it—and you must *believe* you will overcome it. It's that sense of constant forward movement I believe is encapsulated in the words "voy, *I go.*" Every single person who's ever been successful in life has this driving determination to overcome any obstacle to achieve their goal. As Vince Lombardi once said, "Don't tell me how rocky the sea is, just bring in the ship."

I'm not talking about blind optimism. I'm not talking about the ability some people seem to have to be blithely cheerful about their lives no matter what calamity befalls them.

I'm talking about knowing and having faith in your mission. It's about saying, "*This* is my mission. *This* is my goal. *This* is my Grail." People may tell you, "You're nuts to think you can sell your comic strip to the newspapers. Those things are all syndicated. They don't want some crazy strip about a talking daisy on a windowsill. Stick to your day job." They may in fact be right—

but your mission is much greater, your sense of where you can go is clear, and so you don't have to put yourself in the position of debating every negative thought that comes your way. You listen to their objections, you take them in, you may even adapt your strategy if you think they've made a valid point that's useful to you. But you also realize that what's driving you forward is much greater than a single negative comment or reaction. You're on a quest for your own personal Grail. As you progress through the woods, you may come to a tree that has fallen in your path, or a stream that crosses it, or some other challenge or obstacle. You don't turn back at the first sign that your way is blocked. Because you know that if you keep pressing forward—even if that means a temporary setback, having to go around that fallen tree or wading through that stream—you're going to find your Grail.

If you look at any of the successful people you admire—from famous politicians or scientists or doctors to that third-grade teacher who inspired you—you'll see that they have this greater sense of purpose that surpasses the moment, surpasses any minor negative thought or obstacle, and carries them forward. This is the essence of **transcendence.**

Many of us go through life without that greater sense of purpose to give us our direction. Too often we live entirely in the here and now, crossing bananas and milk off our grocery lists, punching in PINs at the ATM, racing to get to the Park & Ride to make the 7:32 train into the city. Too often we live in a state of mind where other people's opinions make us doubt ourselves and our own beliefs. Without belief in yourself and your vision, you may go through your whole life like a little paper boat tossed back and forth on a sea of other people's opinions. You may abandon your own path through the woods and follow someone else's. It's easier to live that way, because someone else has already cleared a path for you. But it will never lead you to your Grail.

I'm not saying you should be completely deaf to the good advice of others. That's foolish, too. I am saying that you need to pick and choose the kinds of advice that will help you achieve your goal. For example, while I have proven myself to be good at envisioning and creating a new business, I am also aware that one of my weaknesses is the financial specifics. I'm not an accountant or a banker. I don't think like an accountant or a banker. I don't even know *how* to think like an accountant or a banker. So if I don't team up with the right accountants and bankers, with people who are good with numbers and financing and the specifics of working out budgets and so on, I'm going to fail to make my vision a reality.

There are two types of people in the world: creators and destroyers. For every Michelangelo, a divinely inspired creator who can bring the most sublime and exquisite sculpture out of unformed stone, there's a destroyer waiting around the corner with a hammer, who'd love to smash that beautiful creation. We see this even in children. At the beach, you watch a child spending hours building a sand castle, completely absorbed in this act of creation. Then another child will come along and out of envy kick and stamp until that beautiful sand castle is reduced to a pile of sand.

Some people carry this destructiveness into adulthood. They can't stand to see someone being creative, being happy, standing out from the crowd. They'll say or do anything negative to tear that person down and prevent them from being successful. Celebrities know this only too well. No sooner do they achieve fame and success than a whole industry of negativity focuses on them with the intent of embarrassing them, negating their success, "cutting them back down to size."

But you don't have to be a movie star to attract this kind of destructive energy. Sometimes all it takes is to be a creative person, someone striving for happiness and self-actualization. You have to learn how to distinguish in your own life between the creators and those destroyers, and not to let that destructive energy contaminate you.

ASSERTING YOUR VISION

The ancient Romans had a saying: *Fortune is the ally of the brave.* I posted that above the door of the first StarMedia office, where the staff would see it every day when they walked in to work. It was 1996; we had almost no capital, and no one believed that the Internet would ever be a force in Latin America. I realized that the only way we were going to make our vision real was by creating our own fortune and making our own opportunities, by going out into the world and aggressively preaching our vision to the people who could help us actualize it.

Vision is the art of seeing the invisible.

—JONATHAN SWIFT

It takes great courage to tell the world about a new idea, a vision that no one has ever had before and that few, at first, believe is realistic. When you're trying to implant a new idea the world, people automatically are going to reject you and tell you it can't be done and call you mad for even thinking it. They'll tell you 101 logical, pragmatic reasons why it won't work. In the end, the only way we became a reality was through our absolute determination to *make* it happen. As they used to say at NASA during the Apollo moon program, failure—ultimate, strategic failure, not small tactical failures along the way—was not an option. Indeed, I was so convinced that our strategic goal was correct that I knew we would be successful, regardless of what happened along the path to that goal. The tactics were almost a nonissue for me, my belief in our ultimate strategic success was so strong.

Remember, **there is no preset, predetermined future. You and the people around you are *creating* the future every day.** There is, therefore, no good reason why you can't make your vision of the future a reality. **If you have absolute faith and are actively projecting that vision into the world and into the minds of the people around you, you** *will* **start to make it a reality.**

I can't stress too many times that to be able to assert your vision, you have to believe it completely and passionately, with every cell of your being. You have to feel that certainty and confidence in order to project it. If you're unsure of your vision yourself, you'll convey that self-doubt to others. If you don't convey total faith in your vision, why should they buy into it? I don't mean you have to be an overbearing, pompous juggernaut of optimism. But if you project doubt, you'll instill doubt.

This is a lesson I learned the hard way. In my earliest meetings in Hollywood to discuss my plans for VOY, I allowed my insecurities to weaken my message. Hollywood was new territory for me, I felt like an outsider from back east, and I came off rather shy and hesitant. "I know my plans might sound a little crazy . . ."

They didn't need to hear that! I was there to inspire them to join me on this journey, not to reinforce any preconceived notions they may have of its craziness. And it wasn't even authentic on my part. I personally had no doubts about my vision. But I went into those early meetings worrying that *they* would have doubts—and then I agreed with them!

After the first couple of missteps, I learned to project my vision in a more assertive and authentic way. I simply told them what the future was going to be, and offered them the opportunity to help me create it. By projecting truthfully how very confident I was about it, I made it much easier for them to believe in and participate in it. I remember one meeting where I was describing a VOY television show, and the woman across the conference table said, "That sounds fabulous. When did it air? How did I miss it?" I had to explain that it hadn't aired—it hadn't even been produced yet. I could just envision it so clearly that she'd thought I was describing an existing program. By the end of that meeting, she was totally prepared to help me make it a reality.

Sometimes getting other people to see what you envision means persuading them to adjust their focus. Did you know that most comets and asteroids that have been identified were not spotted by professional astronomers at their giant telescopes but by amateurs? That's because the professional astronomers simply aren't looking for them. They train their instruments on precise, and usually distant, phenomena—faraway galaxies, a specific pulsar, and so on. They're looking at a tiny fragment of the sky, in a most methodical way. It's the thousands of amateurs around the world, scanning the heavens more randomly, who are almost always the ones who happen upon the comets and asteroids hurtling through nearby space.

Selling your vision to others can be like that. They're so busy looking at the world in their own specific way that it's hard for them to refocus their eyes and their minds—especially if your vision is, for them, something new under the heavens.

REVIEW

- There is no objective truth. There is only subjective reality—a reality you can envision and then make real.

- There are two kinds of belief that drive successful people to their goals: reasoned belief and passionate belief.

- Successful people all exhibit the same relentless determination. Regardless of what gets in your way, regardless of any barrier, you must overcome it—and you must *believe* you will overcome it.

- There is no preset, predetermined future. You and the people around you are *creating* the future every day. If you have absolute faith in your vision, and you are actively projecting that vision into the world and into the minds of the people around you, you *will* start to make that vision a reality.

EXERCISE : Practicing Self-Confidence

To assert your vision in the world, you must believe in it—and in yourself. Some people are lucky in that they seem to be born with assertive, self-confident personalities. Most of us are not. Even some of the most successful people in history have been plagued by self-doubt, or shyness, or a terror of presenting their vision to others. But they learned how to get over those doubts and fears, and so can you.

Here are two easy beginner's techniques you can use to help you to develop a feeling of confidence in yourself and your vision. You can practice them at home, in private. Practice them daily, and pretty soon you should experience a difference in how you present yourself and your ideas to others.

1. BE YOUR OWN CHAMPION

One of the biggest psychological obstacles to asserting yourself in public is not the way others see you but the way you see yourself—your own feelings of inadequacy, your fears, the way you doubt your own abilities. It's not that others lack confidence in you, but that you lack confidence in yourself.

Instead of tearing yourself down, try building yourself up. Every day when you get up, look at yourself in the mirror and give yourself a confidence-building pep talk. Congratulate yourself for something you did well yesterday, even if it was something seemingly small and no one else seemed to notice. "When that customer started to get angry, you did a really good job of defusing the situation." Or "That extra lap you swam yesterday was a real milestone. Just last week you wouldn't have believed you could do it. Excellent."

At first you may feel silly talking to yourself, but stick with it. Give yourself a little pat on the back every morning before you start your day. You'll gradually feel your self-confidence growing. The more you can find to praise about yourself, the easier you'll find it to counteract your negative thoughts or attitudes.

2. SEE YOURSELF AS A WINNER

Projecting a positive, confident image is of critical importance when you're trying to inspire others to work with you toward a goal. If you project doubt or negativity, others will surely pick

(continued)

up on it. Before you can inspire them to see you as a winner and a leader, you must be able to see yourself that way.

Before making a presentation to others, it can be very useful to picture your presentation in your mind—and imagine it going over successfully. See it in as much detail as you can. Picture the setting—a conference room, your supervisor's office, wherever it will be. Imagine your audience—see their faces, how they're dressed, how they're sitting. Now practice going through your presentation, including every step as you've prepared it. See yourself making this presentation calmly, confidently, projecting your optimism onto the audience and feeling their positive response.

The more times you can repeat this "practice run" before the date of the actual presentation, the more confident and relaxed you'll be when the time comes—and the greater the chances for a successful result.

Project and Transform

*I figured that if I said it enough, I would convince
the world that I really was the greatest.*

—MUHAMMAD ALI

*I*n the sixteenth century, England's Queen
Elizabeth passed laws regulating the kinds of clothing and jewelry her subjects could wear. No one but nobles and royalty, she
decreed, was allowed to wear such materials as silk or satin, ermine fur, or gold and silver brocade.

These kinds of decrees, known as sumptuary laws, have been
enforced in almost all cultures at one time or another. Their purpose is often to reinforce class distinctions in fashion. In Elizabeth's time, the merchant class had grown quite wealthy, and they
could afford to dress up in the fancy outfits they saw nobles and
royalty wearing. The Queen and her nobles were outraged to see
mere shopkeepers dressing as well as (or even better than) they
could, so she put a stop to it by enforcing, in effect, a national
dress code.

Elizabeth wasn't simply making a fashion statement. If a duke
was indistinguishable in public from a wealthy shopkeeper, it suggested that the entire order of English society was eroding. Nobles and royals were supposed to be indisputably at the top of the
social pyramid, in a class totally separated from and well above

the commoners. If you let lowborn merchants look and act like dukes and princesses, it implied a lack of respect for this rigid hierarchy—with far-reaching repercussions. Who knew what the commoners would want to do next? Maybe take over running the country?

As it turned out, Elizabeth was right to be concerned. It would take another two hundred years and more, but throughout Europe the common people did eventually take over, deposing their kings or reducing them to figureheads.

There are good reasons why kings and queens wear jeweled crowns and ermine cloaks. There's a reason up-and-coming businessmen like to flash their gold Rolexes. It was no accident that the senators of Rome were put out when Julius Caesar started to wear his all-purple togas.

Everyone creates an image of himself in the world, whether he intends to or not. This image affects your every encounter in the world. If you project a negative image, its impact will be poisonous for you. Crafting and projecting a positive self-image, on the other hand, can transform you into someone who controls situations and commands respect. Every great leader knows this. To become a leader, someone who inspires confidence and cooperation in others, you must think and act like a leader. Eventually, this projection becomes actual transformation.

The things we choose to drape on our bodies are highly symbolic visual cues. There is a direct correlation between how you dress and the status you claim for yourself—and the status others are willing to give you. In this society, we're brought up to believe that clothing and appearance are superficial—that it's "what's inside that counts." And this is true, of course. Yet you cannot ignore that the way you present yourself sends all kinds of messages about "what's inside." And those messages you're sending have a powerful effect on how people receive you, and therefore on your ability to assert your will in the world. How you look and act—not just your clothes, but your manners, your deportment, the way you speak, even your posture—all send conscious or unconscious signals about who you are, where you come from, and where you're going in life. They're part of the whole package you present to others. How you "package" yourself can either enhance or limit your ability to assert your vision and will in the world.

We all implicitly understand this. It's no accident that books like John T. Molloy's *Dress for Success* and *Miss Manners' Guide to Excruciatingly Correct Behavior* are enormous sellers. The popular TV show *Queer Eye for the Straight Guy*, in which experts give your average American male slob a complete makeover from shoes to hair to home furnishings, is not a "fashion show" in any real sense; rather, it is based on the understanding that improving how a man projects himself maximizes his ability to function successfully in society.

Growing up poor as I did, I was always painfully conscious of my secondhand clothes. Especially in high school, when issues of social status are so magnified, my shabby clothes were yet another way of marking me as an "outsider," somehow "different" from and "not as good as" my well-dressed fellow students.

Early in VOY's development I flew from New York to Hollywood to meet with studio executives about creating VOY television programming. The instant I entered the conference room, I realized I was dressed wrong for this meeting. It wasn't that I was not dressed well—I was wearing a suit and tie. It was precisely the way one dresses for a business meeting in New York. But I could see right away that I was overdressed for a business meeting in Hollywood. The studio execs were all dressed California casual—very nice shirts and slacks, but no jacket or tie. In their world, I looked like an uptight, conservative New Yorker.

The remedy wasn't as simple as loosening the knot of my tie. The way I was dressed would still send these Hollywood producers the unintended message that I was not one of them. Simply by the way I was dressed, I had unconsciously made my job of enlisting these people in my cause a little harder.

I returned to New York determined not to make that mistake again. At the same time, I don't know a lot about fashion and hadn't a clue how to dress myself in that California, stylish-but-comfortable way. I asked a friend who knows about fashion to advise. She went shopping with me for a more appropriate wardrobe. It was a fascinating experience for someone who's not terribly fashion-conscious. First she had me pick out clothes that I liked. Everything I chose she turned down as too dull and buttoned-down. Then she picked out a wardrobe that was completely different from the way I normally dressed—more color, richer fabrics, and a looser, more casual drape.

I was amazed over the following weeks at how this new wardrobe transformed the way people reacted to me, both in New York and in Hollywood. I found people warming to me much more quickly than they did in my normal uptight-businessman attire. Women everywhere were giving me compliments on my clothes. That had *never* happened to me before.

The change in the way people reacted to my outward appearance brought about some striking inner changes for me. I felt much more confident. I stood out in a way I never had before, and found that I liked it. The effects went much deeper than simply "dressing for success." **There's a direct and powerful psychological correlation between how you look, how you feel about yourself, and how people treat you.**

If, like me, you don't trust your own fashion sense, a friend who "gets" you and understands how you're trying to translate your inner self to the world can be your adviser, your "mirror."

You can easily consult the fashion industry itself by picking up a copy of a magazine like *GQ* or *Vogue* and flipping through the ads to find outfits that make sense for you and the way you want to present yourself. You don't need to pay top-dollar prices, either—chains like the Gap, as well as the department store in your nearest mall, carry lower-priced versions of the same fashions. And there are books, like the *Chic Simple Dress Smart* series, specifically written to walk you through the basics of building an appropriate, affordable work wardrobe.

How you present yourself in other ways besides your clothing encodes many subtle messages—some of which you may not intend. The examples are easy and obvious. If you slouch, hunch your shoulders, and stare at the ground in public, you're signaling the world that you have low self-esteem. When you slump in a chair, you're telling people you're too lazy to sit up straight. If you speak only in street slang and vulgarities, you're showing that you don't have very high social aspirations for yourself. A limp-fish handshake instantly signals a weak character.

If you think knowing which fork is the salad fork or how to use a napkin is just social artifice, think again. Etiquette and manners are the distillation of thousands of years of social behavior. And, like it or not, they're also codes of behavior by which people in power identify one another in social settings. It's no accident that often in the job-application process you're asked to have lunch or dinner with your prospective employers. It's not because they think you need a meal. It's because they want to see how you handle yourself in a social environment—whether you're someone they want to have on their team. If you sit there eating with your mouth open and reaching for the other person's water glass, they're going to think you're probably a crass and ill-mannered person in other ways.

Many people lead their lives as though common courtesy

were unimportant. "I don't care whether I'm rude to others. I'm an individual. I'm free. What do I care if some schmuck thinks I'm rude?"

You see people acting this way all the time. I was recently on a flight from Los Angeles to New York, and the man in the seat ahead of me spent the entire flight acting like a rude pig to the flight attendants and his fellow passengers. For hours this man spread negativity and unhappiness to everyone around him. When we landed, I gave him a hand getting his bag down from the luggage rack, and he not only didn't thank me, he didn't even acknowledge my presence. At that moment, believe me, I was sorry I had helped him. I'm sure there are a lot of other people this man has been rude to in his life who feel the same way. Eventually, if you're rude to others, it *will* come back to haunt you.

Juan Carlos, the King of Spain, was once late for an interview with a journalist, and when he arrived he apologized profusely for his tardiness. The journalist was startled that the king thought he needed to apologize to a mere reporter. Juan Carlos replied that it was precisely because he is the king that he constantly strives to show respect and courtesy to everyone. It is his duty to show his people, by his example, how important it is that they respect one another. If the king tries to be on time and apologizes when he's tardy, shouldn't the rest of us be as courteous?

It's extremely easy to learn the basic codes of etiquette and manners. Your nearest bookstore or library is guaranteed to carry a variety of books, like the Miss Manners series, that explain it all. There are also "business etiquette" books that offer tips on how to act at a job interview, in a business meeting, and so on.

This may all seem shallow and trivial, but **unless your ultimate goal is to become a hermit on a remote mountaintop, how you interface with the rest of the world will have a huge impact on your ultimate success or failure in getting what you want out**

of life. Being equipped to make others feel comfortable and accepting of you so that you can communicate your ideas to them is a crucial skill. Being polite and courteous to others is in your own self-interest and makes it easier to enlist their aid and support when you need it.

THE POWER OF PROJECTION

Nowhere do we see more respect for the power of projection than in the field of brand marketing. It's no accident that in English the same word, "branding," refers to the identifying mark indelibly burned into the hides of cattle and a corporate product whose identity is permanently seared into our brains.

The 1950s were a golden era in brand marketing, a period when many marketing and advertising techniques were pioneered to push a galaxy of new products in a booming consumer environment. Today, competing brands of laundry detergents try to demonstrate that they're more effective than the others, more environmentally safe, more "concentrated," and so on. Not so in the 1950s. Back then, all laundry detergents were basically the same; it was only the packaging and marketing that distinguished your brand from your competitors'. Marketing departments and advertising agents labored feverishly and created many ingenious campaigns to make Biz look like a more desirable product than Duz, or to prompt the housewife to prefer Cheer over Tide. Cheer, for example, experimented with different colors of soap powders. Cheer detergent is blue today because women fifty years ago decided they liked blue crystals better than red or yellow. Different fragrances were also added to detergents to get users to prefer one over the others.

The "soap opera" is another direct result of the detergent marketing wars of the 1950s, as each brand associated itself with a particular daytime drama in an attempt to distinguish itself from its competitors: One brand sponsored *Guiding Light*, another sponsored *As the World Turns*, and so on.

You'll note that none of this branding had anything to do with making one detergent *work* better than the others; it was purely a war of packaging, projection, and image.

Believe it or not, brand marketing isn't always so cynical-sounding. When I worked at Ogilvy & Mather, one of my accounts was Unilever's Dove soap. Like laundry detergents, most brands of soap bars are the same. The consumer goes to the supermarket and there are forty or fifty brands of soap on the shelves. The marketer's job is to get that consumer to choose his brand on a regular basis. It's very difficult. People give almost no thought to soap, except at that specific moment when they're in that aisle of the supermarket. The marketer has to make his brand of soap so relevant to the consumer's life that he or she will remember to pick it up at that moment.

Dove has in fact managed to distinguish itself from all other soaps; everyone knows that Dove is "one-quarter moisturizing cream." That's a real, tangible benefit to the user that no other brand of soap can claim. And by literally "branding" that benefit on the minds of consumers, Dove's marketers have made the brand the single most successful soap on the planet.

Younger readers may not remember this, but there was a time not so very long ago when a glass of water was the most humble, most common thing in the world. It was (more or less) odorless, tasteless, and colorless, and ubiquitously available at the twist of a faucet. Nobody, at least in the industrialized world, gave water a second thought.

Then the French bottlers Perrier and Evian achieved the most remarkable and formerly unthinkable feat: They transformed simple water into a prestige commodity. Ingeniously projecting an image of bottled water as an accoutrement of the rich and fa-mous, a lifestyle accessory with a splash of European panache, Evian literally created a market where none had existed before. A bottle of simple water became an image-enhancer that in its way was as much a status symbol as a Jaguar and a Rolex—but a lot more affordable. Bottled water was chic, bottled water was smart, bottled water was "classy."

When one company invents new territory the way Evian did, many others are sure to follow. Today, there are dozens of "de-signer" waters, all jockeying to project a convincing image that their water is somehow "better" than their competitors', or at least more hip and fashionable.

None has projected its image more cleverly than Fiji Water. A small bottler founded in 1996, Fiji does no traditional advertis-ing, yet it has successfully eclipsed Evian as the preferred water of the "in crowd." It has accomplished this through sponsorship of chic events like New York's Fashion Week, by insinuating it-self as the "official" bottled water at famous upscale restaurants in Manhattan and Los Angeles, and by shipping cases to movie stars, TV stars, and other celebrities, who dutifully flash the Fiji bottle when the paparazzi are snapping their pictures.

On top of that brilliant "guerrilla marketing campaign," Fiji Water, unlike some of its competitors, really does come from a pure spring on one of the Fiji Islands. So it can actually claim to be not only hipper, but better than the rest.

Even a gigantic and globally successful corporation like Mc-Donald's understands and relies on the power of projection. If you could go back and look at McDonald's ads from thirty or forty years ago, you'd see many images of happy American fam-ilies devouring juicy burgers and crispy, mouthwatering fries. If you look at McDonald's commercials today, however, you'll no-tice something curious: There's not a hamburger in sight. The word "hamburger" isn't even mentioned. If space aliens monitored today's McDonald's ads, they'd have no clue that it's a hamburger chain. With all the attacks on fast food as a "cause" of obesity over the last several years, McDonald's has learned to project a new image, one that completely downplays its "unhealthy" products like burgers and fries for supposedly more "healthy" items like Chicken McNuggets and Happy Meals (which are ingeniously cross-promoted with Disney films, the epitome of kid-friendly, "wholesome" Americana).

Some of these may sound like cynical examples of corporate marketing hijinks, but we can all take a lesson from them. You are facing a marketplace as well. **As you proceed to your personal goal—whether that's a business venture, or a better job, or fulfilling your dream of becoming a filmmaker or dancer—there's a high probability that you're going to have to "sell" yourself and your vision to others.** How you package yourself, and the image you project, can be crucial to the success of your endeavors.

A LEADER PROJECTS STRENGTH

When two competing young male chimpanzees of equal size and strength run into each other in a jungle clearing, a very curious and interesting bit of theater ensues. Neither one wants to provoke a fight with a competitor who's roughly his size, since there's a fifty-fifty chance he'll lose. And to lose the fight would mean not only the chance of a life-threatening injury, but much worse, a reduction of status within the tribe. For a young male chimpanzee, status within the group is everything. If he can carefully maintain and advance his place within the group, a young male may someday get to be its leader, the "alpha male." And, to paraphrase Mel Brooks's famous line, it's good to be the alpha male in a chimpanzee tribe. The alpha male gets the best food, the softest rest-ing place, the first shot at the females, and many other perks. (He also inherits all the stress, responsibility, and physical danger of being the leader, but young chimps, like many young executives racing up the corporate ladder, don't seem to concern themselves with this darker side of success.)

So the two young chimps, each confronting an opponent of roughly equal strength, are careful not to go into any show of aggression when they meet. Not wanting to provoke a fight when there's an equal chance they'll lose, they don't beat their chests, bare their teeth, flail their arms in the air—in short, they don't "go ape." Instead, they both draw themselves up to their full height, adopt the most dignified stature they can—and stand there, still as statues, staring at each other impassively and apparently unconcernedly for as long as they can hold the pose. Then they simply turn and quietly go their separate ways. They live to fight another day.

Later, when each young ape thinks he is alone in the forest, unobserved by the rest of the tribe, he'll relax and let all the stress of that meeting flow out of him. He'll tremble with fear and bare his teeth in an anguished grimace. He'll pound the ground and shake branches. It took an enormous exertion of discipline for him to repress any sign of that tension in his public confrontation with his rival. Alone, this is how he lets it all out.

During the peak of his power as ruler of Nazi Germany, Adolf Hitler was infamous for his bullying, browbeating behavior when addressing other political figures. He would appear to be supremely confident in his own superiority and that of the German people. No one who suffered through one of these psychologically abusive meetings with Der Führer came away with any inkling that Hitler experienced the slightest self-doubt or had ever known a momentary lapse of self-confidence.

But for Hitler, like those young chimps, it was all theatrics, and it came at the cost of great emotional stress. Alone with his closest supporters after one of these meetings, Hitler would often literally collapse to the floor and suffer bizarre fits of weeping and sobbing. All the anxiety and self-doubt he'd repressed in public came pouring out of him in private.

The world has never come closer to World War III and nuclear destruction than during the Cuban missile crisis of 1962. The Soviet Union was installing missile bases in Cuba, a scant ninety miles from Florida. It was an outrageously provocative act, clearly meant to test the courage of the young President John F. Kennedy.

Kennedy knew that if he showed any weakness or hesitation, the Soviets would feel free to wreak havoc all over the world. So he stood firm. He demanded that the Soviets remove the missiles. In the extremely tense showdown that ensued, Kennedy went on national TV to address the American people. He projected an image of calm strength and indomitable resolve that helped to quell the mounting state of panic that gripped the nation. It also helped to convince the Soviets that he meant business, and they finally backed down, dismantling the missile bases.

In private, Kennedy and his closest advisers agonized over the tremendous risks of having this face-off with the Soviets. He knew full well that his decisions might plunge the world into a nuclear nightmare. But he was also confident that he was making the correct decision. This confidence gave him the resolve to carry it through successfully.

Anyone who's ever been in a position of leadership, from the captain of a high school soccer team to a corporate CEO to the president, learns how to project calm, strength, and confidence, especially in moments of the highest stress and crisis. A successful leader keeps his eye on the prize, and through his example keeps his team (staff, colleagues, citizens, etc.) focused on the ultimate goal. He seems most calm and focused at precisely those moments when everyone around him is ready to panic. Inwardly, he's feeling the stress just as much as the people under him—probably more so, in fact, since he's ultimately responsible for leading them through it. But he doesn't show that. By projecting strength and optimism, he inspires and instills it in those around him.

In the early stages of StarMedia, when we were on the brink of running out of cash all the time and I was flying all over the country trying to convince venture capitalists to get behind this new vision of mine, I made a point of being very visible in the office whenever I could. I would walk around to everyone's desk, say hello to everyone, smile, joke around a little with them. I knew they were concerned that we could fail any day. They were all looking to me—my body language, my apparent mood—to judge how scared they should be. I knew we *weren't* going to fail, and I made sure they could see that in me. By projecting my faith in our ultimate success, I not only calmed their fears but I helped them to stay focused on the tasks at hand and not be distracted by fear—which, in the end, helped to ensure our success.

That's how leadership, the power of optimism, and the power of projection work together. They're self-reinforcing. **If you have confidence in your vision, and you project that, you inspire those around you so that together you can achieve your shared goal.**

REVIEW

- There's a direct and powerful psychological correlation between how you look, how you feel about yourself, and how people treat you.

- As you proceed to your personal goal, there's a high probability that you're going to have to "sell" yourself and your vision to others. How you package yourself, and the image you project, can be crucial to the success of your endeavors.

- A leader projects strength. If you have confidence in your vision, and you project that, you inspire those around you so that together you can achieve your shared goal.

E X E R C I S E :   What Image Do I Project?

The image you project to the world can be critical to your ability to achieve your goals. When meeting strangers who can help or hinder you, first impressions can make all the difference. Some psychological studies suggest that in first meetings, the impression you make depends 55 percent on how you look, 38 percent on how you speak, and only 7 percent on what you actually say.

What kind of image do you think you project to the world? Extroverted or introverted? Casual or uptight? Talkative or quiet? Neat or sloppy? Strong, self-confident, comfortable meeting others? Or shy and insecure?

The truth is, we're not always sure what kind of image we project. It can be a great help to have a friend we trust act as our "mirror," and identify if there are discrepancies between the image we *think* we project and the image others actually see.

That's the purpose of this exercise. Answer the questions below as truthfully as you can. Then show your answers to a trusted friend and ask him or her to tell you honestly how accurate your answers seem. If there are aspects of your image that could use work—your clothes, your posture, your handshake, your manners, and so on—this exercise can help identify them.

1. In general, my clothing is (circle one):
    Neat   Sloppy

2. I generally dress in a style that is (circle one):
    Conservative   Casual   Provocative   Gaudy

3. My hair and grooming tend to be (circle one):
    Neat   Casual   Unkempt

4. In general, my posture is (circle one):
    Stiff   Relaxed   Slouched

5. True or False: I seem confident and at ease around strangers.

6. True or False: I have a firm, confident handshake.

(continued)

7. True or False: I look the other person in the eye when we are talking.

8. True or False: I generally express myself clearly and directly.

9. I tend to use speech that is (circle one):

   Formal

   Casual but correct

   Slangy and vulgar

10. When I am nervous or meeting someone for the first time, I sometimes have a tendency to (circle all that apply):

    Stutter

    Mumble

    Speak too quickly

    None of the above

11. When I am nervous or meeting someone for the first time, I sometimes have a tendency to (circle all that apply):

    Bite my nails

    Drum my fingers

    Hide my face behind my hands or hair

    Hunch my shoulders

    Tap my feet

    Laugh too loudly

    None of the above

12. In a group, I tend to be (circle one):

    Outgoing and engaged   Shy and withdrawn

13. In a group, I tend to (circle one):

    Take a leadership role   Be part of the crowd

14. In a group, I tend to be (circle one):

    Bossy and demanding   Cooperative and compromising

15. True or False: I am good at focusing on another person and making them feel I am listening to them and care about what they are saying.

16. True or False: I have a tendency to interrupt when others are speaking.

17. In general, I seem (circle one):
    Polite and courteous   Abrupt and rude

18. In general, I seem (circle one):
    Friendly and approachable   Cold and distant

19. True or False: I have good table manners.

Be Persistent

Aviation is proof that given the will, we have the capacity to achieve the impossible.

—EDDIE RICKENBACKER

THE WRIGHT STUFF

I've logged millions of frequent-flyer miles over the course of my career so far. When I was traveling all over Latin America for AT&T, there were periods when I spent more time in the air than on the ground. I've crisscrossed the continental United States more times than I can count.

Flying has become so routine and even boring for many of us that it's hard to remember it's only been a few decades since air travel became a common means of transportation—and only a century since the Wright brothers made man's first controlled flight in a powered aircraft on December 17, 1903. What they did that day, Microsoft founder Bill Gates has said, was the greatest technological leap forward for mankind since the invention of writing.

Men had dreamed of flying for thousands of years before 1903. The earliest attempt to fly we know about was in 850 B.C.—roughly three thousand years ago. A man attached wings to his arms and jumped off a temple of Apollo. He crashed and died. (Apollo was the ancient Greek god whose chariot was thought to pull the sun across the sky. NASA named the first manned flights to the moon the Apollo program.)

The history of man's attempts to fly is an unbroken line of failure and disaster from then until 1783, when a Frenchman, Montgolfier, made the first manned flight in a hot-air balloon. For twenty-five hundred years, man tried to give himself wings—and often died trying. Some of the greatest scientific minds in history, like Leonardo da Vinci, were obsessed with the challenge of inventing flying machines. Others were crackpots, dreamers, lone amateur inventors who built themselves wings of wood and cloth and feathers, clambered up to the top of a hill or the roof of a barn, and leaped into the unknown. And for thousands of years, time and time again, they crashed, often fatally.

And yet people kept trying. The dream of flight was so compelling that men kept strapping on their homemade wings and jumping off high places despite the thousands of failures before them. They also persisted despite the jeers, disapproval, and even religious condemnation of society. Flying was generally thought to be impossible, and any man who believed he could fly was considered insane. In the Middle Ages, Christians even believed that attempting to fly was evil. "If God had wanted man to fly," the saying goes, "He would have given him wings." For a long time, Christians truly believed this. The sky was the domain of flying demons and devils, and anyone who wanted to join them up there must be a heretic.

But the dreamers persisted. In the late 1700s, hot air balloons gave them their first taste of what it felt like to float above the treetops and church steeples. At the turn of the twentieth century, the Wright brothers flew the first practical gliders ever designed, then added a gas-powered engine and controls, creating the world's first airplane. Within ten short years, the sky seemed to be filled with small, sputtering airplanes of wood and canvas. World War I (1914–1918) was the first war in human history to be fought in the skies as well as on the ground, and the heroic feats of "flying aces" like Eddie Rickenbacker and Baron von Richthofen ("the Red Baron") are legendary. Commercial air travel was born and grew in the 1920s and 1930s. Since the 1960s, affordable, readily available air travel is taken for granted. The skies are no longer the domain of flying demons or even flying aces; hundreds of millions of people fly, all around the world.

But we'd all still be stuck on the ground if all those dreamers, inventors, madmen, and heretics hadn't persisted through all those centuries in leaping into the unknown, despite the huge risks, despite the widespread belief that flying was impossible.

As you embark on your own flight, your own leap into the unknown, there will no doubt be skeptics and naysayers who tell you that your goal is impossible, too. You'll be told you're crazy, a dreamer, and that you don't have the skills or talent to achieve your dream. You'll doubt yourself. You'll know bitter disappointment and setbacks. You'll confront obstacles that seem insurmountable.

Successful people are the ones who persist in the face of all that negativity. They achieve the "impossible."

RIDING THE ROLLER COASTER

Anyone who's ever started up a new business will tell you it's a roller coaster. If you chart the growth of any new business venture, from a new corner grocery to a new global conglomerate formed by the merger of AOL and Time Warner, only in the very rarest incidence will that chart be a neat, straight uphill line from rags to riches. In almost every case that chart's going to look more like the Himalayan Mountains, a jagged succession of sharp peaks and steep valleys. Even for that giant conglomerate, the swings from highs to lows can come daily. Today you're cracking open the Cristal to celebrate the merger. The next morning, you're ready to hang yourself when your new stock plummets on Wall Street.

As you start out on your personal venture, whatever that is— to find Mr. Right, or open a restaurant, or become a documentary filmmaker—I can almost guarantee you that your path will not be straight and level. There will be peaks of joy and valleys of despair. You'll meet Mr. Right at "Rockin' With the Lord" today; tomorrow his employer will transfer him to an office in Taiwan. This week you'll open your restaurant to large crowds and fabulous reviews; next week your entire clientele will go on vacation and you'll be empty every night.

To weather the ups and downs takes *persistence*, and the firm belief that if you've set your course toward the right goal you will eventually succeed. At StarMedia we experienced violent shifts from great success to what seemed like utter failure all the time. Very early on, I learned not to allow the good days and bad jerk me around. I didn't emotionally oscillate with our changing daily fortunes. I knew where we were aiming ourselves, and every Friday I evaluated the week by how much closer to or farther away from our goal we had gotten. Where were we Monday, and where are we today?

I had a colleague at StarMedia in those rough-and-tumble early months who simply could not think that way. He reacted to every good day with overblown ebullience, and every downturn plunged him into the deepest despair. At least twice a week he would have a small meltdown. For me, because I liked and respected him, the challenge was not to let his frequent bouts of fear and depression pollute me.

As you pursue your own goal, you need to keep focused on

the future you've envisioned, the future you're creating for yourself every day—even on the worst of the bad days. You need to make the *power of optimism* work for you on those bad days especially.

THERE ARE NO EXCUSES—ONLY CHALLENGES

It matters if you just don't give up.

—STEPHEN J. HAWKING

Life presents us all with challenges. Every path is strewn with obstacles. Every growth chart has its jagged peaks and valleys. But only you can prevent yourself from reaching your Grail. And you will never achieve happiness or success if you allow yourself to turn obstacles and challenges into *excuses for failure*—or worse, for not even trying.

Sadly, many people do just that. They decide that the deck is stacked against them from the start because of their race or ethnicity, or because they're making minimum wage, or because they're female, or they have only a third-grade education, or because they're deaf. People offer many excuses for failing to live up to their full potential. But that's all they are—excuses. Yes, racism, classism, sexism do exist. Many people do start out life with severe disadvantages. But you never hear successful people speaking of their disadvantages as excuses—only as challenges they overcame on their way to success.

I faced my own obstacles. I came to the United States with no money and speaking not one word of English. In addition to poverty, I suffered active ethnic biases that displayed themselves—in school and elsewhere—as a constant, ongoing facet of my experience growing up. I was scorned as a "fat spic." My junior high school gym coach refused to pronounce my name for three years. He would only call me by this joking nickname, Spijetus. It was his version of Espuelas: Spijetus. Still, despite being poor, despite being jeered at for my ethnicity, I never saw myself as a "victim" or "disadvantaged." It just made me strive harder to succeed. I can understand how people grow up in that kind of environment and feel it's a brand, an indelible stigma. I know how difficult it is to break through that. But **you can't let someone else's prejudice be the limiting factor in your life.** You have to turn that situation around, to make it a source of strength instead of weakness. That's your challenge in life, and there is no progress without challenge.

No matter how "disadvantaged" you believe you are, no matter how huge the obstacles in your path may seem to you, there are people who have struggled much harder than you will have to, and shouldered burdens just as great as or greater than yours—and did not allow any of that to become an excuse for failure.

Recently I met the Garcia family of Venice Beach, California. Rogelio Garcia came to the United States from Oaxaca, Mexico, in the late 1970s without a penny in his pocket. He and his wife of more than twenty years, Yolanda, have worked tirelessly to be the best parents they can be to their three children, and to secure for them the best educations possible. Yolanda worked in factories and cleaned homes. Rogelio was a dishwasher and a meat cutter.

In 1988, Rogelio Garcia was laid off from his job. Unable to find other work, he turned to what many of us might consider the lowest, least dignified labor imaginable. Since then, he and Yolanda have eked out a meager living pulling recyclable cans, bottles, and plastic from garbage cans and dumpsters. They work fourteen hours a day, seven days a week, 365 days a year, and earn about $15,000 annually.

The Garcias rent a tiny apartment that costs them $500 a month. They have to collect roughly 16,000 cans a month just to pay that. And yet every month for years they sent $400—a third of what they earned—to their two children in college.

Yes, despite being "trash pickers" and "dumpster divers," despite earning far below what's considered the poverty level in the

United States, the Garcias have been putting their children through college. "For me this is not a sacrifice," Yolanda told me. "For me, this is my obligation."

In 2002, Rogelio Jr. graduated from MIT with a degree in aerospace engineering. His sister, Adrianne, is earning a degree in marketing at the University of California–Riverside. The third child, Angel, has started college, and Rogelio Jr. now helps pay for it.

The life of Rogelio and Yolanda Garcia is obviously not a fairy-tale "rags to riches" story. It's a life of crushing poverty and grueling, ceaseless labor. Yet in spite of those burdens, they are achieving their goal of putting their children through college and assuring them a better life. As parents, they are a sterling success. "Nothing is impossible," Yolanda says. "You *can* do it."

Stephen J. Hawking is widely considered the most brilliant theoretical physicist since Albert Einstein. His work on black holes and on the big bang theory of the birth of the universe represents huge leaps forward in our understanding of the cosmos. He is also the most highly celebrated physicist of our day, not only in the scientific community but in popular culture as well—his book *A Brief History of Time* was a huge best-seller ("I have sold more books on physics than Madonna has on sex," he once joked), and he was even a guest star on *Star Trek*. Yet he had to overcome an enormous physical challenge to achieve what he has.

Born in Oxford, Britain, in 1942, Hawking did not distinguish himself academically in his early school years. He was better known for his awkward manner and his lisp, which fellow students dubbed "Hawkingese." Studying physics at Oxford University, he stood out more for his intuitive grasp of theory than for his diligent scholarship. He graduated with an undistinguished record.

It was in 1962, during his final year at Oxford, at the age of twenty, that Hawking noticed he was becoming increasingly "clumsy." It was the first sign that he was suffering from Lou Gehrig's disease (amyotrophic lateral sclerosis), an incurable and virtually always fatal disease of the nervous system that robs the sufferer of all muscle control. The mind is not affected and there is no physical pain, but the body becomes entirely paralyzed and wastes away. Hawking was not expected to live long enough to complete his postgraduate studies.

And yet he is still alive today, the father of three children, and has revolutionized the science of physics. In his early years of battling the disease, which gradually reduced him to an emaciated figure in a wheelchair, he fought depression and despair to display an astounding grasp of theoretical cosmology, earn his Ph.D. with highest honors—and marry the woman he loved. He became a highly distinguished professor at Cambridge University, taking a position previously held by Sir Isaac Newton, and began to prove himself one of the most original and influential minds of his generation.

When he lost the power of speech, he initially communicated with others through an extraordinarily laborious process: They would hold up a chart of the alphabet and point to each letter in turn, and he would raise his eyebrows—one of the few parts of his body he could still control—at each correct letter. In this way, he "spoke" one letter at a time, painstakingly building each word and sentence. Today, he uses a computerized speech synthesizer.

Now in his sixties, Hawking has far outlived the expectations of his doctors, and is firmly established in the company of Einstein, Newton, and Galileo as one of the greatest scientific minds in history.

Winston Churchill gave some of the most inspiring speeches in history, in spite of—or perhaps because of—a speech impediment. As a young member of Parliament, his embarrassment over his lisp rendered him all but speechless. When it was his turn to address that august body, he would mumble, lose track of what he was saying, and end his talks abruptly, covering his face with his hands in shame. He tried special dentures that somewhat corrected his lisp, but they were so painful and frustrating that he was known to fling them across a room in anger.

Later in his career, Churchill learned to make his lisp work for him instead of against him. His peculiar manner of speaking became one of his hallmarks. People respected him all the more, and maybe listened to him more closely, because of the defect.

Franklin Roosevelt and John F. Kennedy overcame serious physical ailments to be remembered as two of the finest presidents in this country's history. Roosevelt contracted polio as a young man. It left his legs permanently paralyzed, and he was confined to a wheelchair for the rest of his life. Rather than let that stop him, he not only went on to a brilliant political career but became a driving force in the research that all but eliminated polio as a disease in this country. JFK became one of history's best-loved and most inspirational figures despite a life racked by agonizing pain, including chronic back problems that defied torturous surgical interventions, grueling intestinal pains caused by various food allergies, and a life-threatening condition called Addison's disease, a rare dysfunction that causes extreme weakness and fatigue.

Are any obstacles, burdens, or disadvantages in your life greater than those these leaders overcame?

People of African-American, Latin, or Asian heritage often cite racism as an insurmountable obstacle in this country. Believe me, I know the ill effects of racism firsthand. But look around you at all of the people from historically "disadvantaged" groups who have succeeded despite these challenges.

In 1950, Tom Fleming was a young African-American man

in Detroit's inner city. A high school dropout who'd been raised by a grandmother when his parents abandoned him, he could neither read nor write. Those skills didn't count for much among the tough gangs he hung out with on the streets. At seventeen, he had every reason to use the excuses of race, poverty, a troubled home life, and lack of education to give up on ever making something of himself.

In 1992, that same Thomas A. Fleming went to the White House to be handed the National Teacher of the Year Award by the president. He had been singled out from among more than 2.5 million teachers across the country for his exemplary work teaching and providing an example for troubled youth in a Michigan juvenile detention center. "Nobody else wants to touch these kids," a fellow teacher said. "They've become so hardened over the years, there's just no way to get through. But Tom gets through."

Fleming had refused to let his supremely disadvantaged start in life keep him from achieving success. He'd joined the National Guard to learn discipline. He earned his high school equivalency diploma at night school, while also becoming a Baptist minister who specialized in reaching out to Detroit's street youth. After earning a master's degree in special education, he concentrated on providing education and guidance for troubled teens in mental institutions and detention centers.

Some women encounter sexism that holds them back from success. Especially in business, it's much harder for women to achieve their goals, no matter how talented and focused they are. Yet that playing field is becoming more level every day. In 2003, the chairman, CEO, and/or president of Hewlett-Packard, AT&T, Xerox, PepsiCo, Chevron-Texaco, Lucent, Avon, Kraft Foods, Ogilvy & Mather, Universal Pictures, Time Inc., and a number of other large corporations were women. (A majority of StarMedia's senior executives were women.)

Look around at all the women and people of color leading meaningful lives. Not just all the celebrated entrepreneurs, athletes, movie stars, political figures, and business leaders, but the teachers, poets, doctors, lawyers, small-business owners, and loving, successful parents—women and minorities succeeding in all walks of life, all around you. All over the country, people are proving every day that these are not unbreakable roadblocks to success but merely challenges to be overcome.

Remember the image of the mountain. **No one lives a full life without climbing some mountains.** That challenge is different for each of us. It may be something as sinister as racism or as pervasive as self-doubt. Life without mountains to climb would be a terrible bore. Walking your whole life along a straight, flat path with no obstacles or challenges is a form of living death. Embracing the struggle, whatever that is, is part of your mission. It's part of your journey.

To dare is to lose one's footing momentarily.
Not to dare is to lose oneself.
—SØREN KIERKEGAARD

REVIEW

- Successful people are the ones who persist in the face of any negativity. They achieve the "impossible."

- As you pursue your goals, keep focused on the future you've envisioned and are creating for yourself every day—even on the worst of days. Make the *power of optimism* work for you on the bad days especially.

- There are no excuses in life—only challenges. Every path is strewn with obstacles. But only you can prevent yourself from reaching your goals. Don't let someone else's prejudice be the limiting factor in your life. You will never achieve happiness or success if you allow yourself to turn obstacles and challenges into excuses for failure.

- No one lives a full life without climbing some mountains. Life without mountains to climb would be a terrible bore. Walking your whole life along a straight, flat path with no obstacles or challenges is a form of living death. Embracing the struggle, whatever that is, is part of your mission. It's part of your journey.

EXERCISE: What's My Excuse?

Unless you were born into a wealthy and powerful family, and grew up beautiful, gifted, and exceptionally bright, it's terribly easy to come up with excuses for not trying to achieve success and happiness. People who resign themselves to unhappiness and don't even want to try for success use every excuse imaginable. "I wasn't born in this country." "I was born poor." "I got a lousy education." "I'm Latin." "I'm not the right gender." "I'm physically challenged." And on and on and on.

These are real challenges. But they are *not* insurmountable obstacles to personal success and happiness. They are *not* excuses for failure.

Here's a challenge of another kind:

In the space below, write down what it is about you that you believe prevents you from becoming happy and successful—your ethnicity, gender, education, whatever it is.

1. I feel I will never be successful or happy because of:

    _____

    _____

2. Now prove yourself wrong. I guarantee you that for whatever you just wrote, you can find at least one example of someone who succeeded *despite* that challenge. This book offers many examples—the severely disabled scientist, the African-American Teacher of the Year, the female CEO, the penniless immigrant who became a multimillionaire, and many others.

    But don't take my word for it. Do your own research. Explore some history or biography. Scan the daily newspapers. Look around your own community. I guarantee you will find examples of people who overcame whatever it is you consider an insurmountable obstacle in your life. The only difference between those successful people and the people who've resigned themselves to failure is that the successful ones met the challenges and let nothing hold them back.

Be Courageous

Only those who dare to fail greatly
can ever achieve greatly.
— ROBERT KENNEDY

*A*s you pursue your path to success you will inevitably encounter moments of crisis, anxiety, and doubt. Every successful person has experienced the fear of the unknown, of taking great risk, of possible failure. Winston Churchill, in spite of all his accomplishments, suffered from acute depression. He even gave it a name: "The Black Dog."

Churchill was one of the greatest statesmen of the twentieth century. As prime minister of Great Britain during World War II, he was responsible, more than any other single person, for saving Europe from Nazi domination. During his lifetime he inspired millions to great acts of courage; as a hero he continues to influence many people, including me.

He accomplished greatness despite lifelong bouts of depression, fear, and self-doubt so severe that he sometimes could not get out of bed for days on end. Psychologists believe that his tendency toward black moods began early in his life, and may even have been genetic: His father and several other male ancestors suffered from severe depression and mental illness. As a young man Churchill was plagued by the terror that he, too, might be prone to insanity.

With his tendency toward melancholy, Churchill was ill-prepared to weather setbacks in his career. As First Lord of the Admiralty during World War I, he led Britain's armed forces to a disastrous defeat against the Central Powers at Gallipoli, a battle that almost ended his political career. His devoted wife would later say that his depression was so overwhelming, "I thought he would die of grief." It took him literally a decade to recover and go on to become, once again, one of Britain's greatest political leaders.

I believe Churchill was able to overcome all his fears, self-doubts, and shortcomings because he devoted himself one hundred percent to the greater good of Britain and the salvation of Western civilization. Despite the constant attacks by the Black Dog, Churchill felt an unshakable belief that he had been called to lead the British people to victory. By focusing on that goal, he was able to persevere and triumph.

Abraham Lincoln struggled all his life with depression, anxiety attacks, and terrifying nightmares. In the years before he became president, his bouts of melancholy could become so grave that his friends kept him under a suicide watch. Like Churchill, he was eventually able to overcome these tendencies by passionately dedicating himself to a higher goal, nothing less than preserving the United States during the Civil War.

Sir Isaac Newton is honored as one of the most important scientific minds in the history of mankind. He completely revolutionized our understanding of the universe through his genius work on gravity, the movements of the planets, and the properties of light, and he invented an entirely new branch of mathematics, calculus. And yet he, too, was plagued all his life by fear and melancholy so severe that many people simply thought him mad. He suffered terribly from insomnia, hypochondria, and anorexia. He was so paranoid that he hesitated for years before revealing some of his most significant scientific discoveries to the world. And yet, like Churchill and Lincoln, by devoting himself to a higher purpose, a goal that eclipsed his own problems, he accomplished scientific breakthroughs that altered the course of human history.

So many illustrious, creative minds have been tortured by periods of depression, manic depression, and crushing self-doubt that a whole branch of psychology is devoted to studying the possible links between creativity and depression. Beethoven, van Gogh, Edgar Allan Poe, Leo Tolstoy, Charles Dickens, and Sylvia Plath are just a few of the artistic geniuses who knew periods of despondency and hopelessness. (Van Gogh and Plath, famously and tragically, both lost that battle in the end and committed suicide.) More recently, the list of highly successful individuals who have had to overcome debilitating bouts of melancholy and anxiety includes Ted Turner, who more or less invented cable television as we know it, comedienne Roseanne Barr, Olympic diver Greg Louganis, Tipper Gore, and pop singers Sheryl Crow, Alanis Morissette, and, of course, Kurt Cobain (another gifted artist who, sadly, lost the battle and committed suicide).

I'm not citing all these examples to put you, too, in a state of depression. I'm only pointing out that when you doubt yourself, when you are fearful of taking the next step toward your goal, when a setback in your journey temporarily convinces you that you don't have what it takes to succeed, remember that you're in the very best company. **Everyone knows fear. Everyone doubts his or her talents and vision sometimes. Successful people find a way to get around those doubts and persevere.**

Persistence, courage, faith in yourself, relentless determination: These are all characteristics common to successful people. But as the above examples and countless others show, these aren't character traits successful people were lucky enough to be born with. They are *psychological tools successful people learn to use,* often with the greatest difficulty. Successful people are just as prone to fear and doubt as you are—maybe more. Like them, you must have the courage to take the leap into the dark, to move forward into the unknown. As Churchill said, "When you're going through hell, keep going." He tamed the Black Dog and became its master.

DON'T LET FEAR HOLD YOU BACK

Courage is the mastery of fear, not the absence of fear.

—MARK TWAIN

If you do an online search on "mastering fear," you'll find dozens of books, cassette tapes, course programs, and even telephone hot lines being offered to help people learn to cope with their fears and phobias. Clearly, fear is one of the largest factors holding people back from trying to self-actualize. Fear of failure, fear of deviating from the lives they've already established, fear of going it alone.

Fear may be *the* inhibitor of self-actualization. But **you cannot eliminate fear. You can only redirect fear.**

First of all, you must understand that fear is a healthy response. It's built into our nervous system to protect us from danger. When we are confronted with some danger—real or imagined, it doesn't matter—our bodies release several hormones that trigger built-in defense mechanisms. Our adrenaline levels rise, our heartbeat and breathing increase. It's called the fight-or-flight response. Your body is preparing itself either to confront the danger or run from it.

All creatures react the same way when presented with a dangerous situation: They automatically fight or flee. When you raise your hand to swat a fly, the fly buzzes off. The fly doesn't know fear—flies don't feel emotions. Avoiding danger is hard-wired into its nervous system. The same protective behavior is wired into all higher forms of life. In humans, it keeps us from doing foolishly dangerous things. No one considers it cowardice if we don't step in front of a bus or stick our fingers in an electric socket or walk into a yard with a raging pit bull in it.

So I don't advocate ignoring fear and pushing through in spite of it. You have to deal with your fear. Think of it as a sort of mental martial art: You have to redirect the energy someplace.

Courage and fear are connected. Courage is a response to fear, not an absolute value in itself.

There is no avoiding fear, but you can make fear be part of the thrill of life. You manage your fear when you ride on a roller coaster, because you know the situation is under control, so you can rationalize your fear and tell yourself nothing bad will happen. Most of life is a roller coaster—except it doesn't come with all the safety devices.

In battle, all soldiers experience fear. It's a natural response to the danger and horror that surrounds them. **The difference between a hero and a coward isn't that the hero feels no fear. It's that the hero does his duty despite the fear. He learns to control and channel it.** What people despise about cowards is not that they experienced fear but that because of their fear they did not do their duty. This is what Ernest Hemingway meant in his famous saying that courage is "grace under pressure."

The trick isn't refusing to let yourself feel fear—that's impossible. It's not letting fear hold you back. Courage is redirecting fear into productive paths. It's taking that angst, that fearful energy, and saying, "I will *not* be conquered by negative thoughts. I will conquer with positive thoughts. I *will* move forward." It's replacing our natural instinct to flee a fear-inducing situation with the opposite reaction: Instead of fleeing, running away, you move forward.

You can train yourself to redirect your fear. First, you must understand that fear is part of the context of human existence.

Without fear, we would not have survived as a species. If our distant forebears had calmly and fearlessly walked up to pet every predator they encountered, none of us would be here. Luckily for us, they turned and ran like mad.

But the crucial point is that our ancestors didn't merely run and hide every time they heard a predator's footsteps. Had they done that, they would have all starved to death huddling in their caves, and that would have been the end of the species. Man became a predator, too. He learned to compete with the lions, tigers, and bears for food. He developed weapons to defend himself against them. He never lost his healthy fear of and respect for the predators, but he learned to survive and thrive in their midst.

You must also learn to analyze what you fear. There's rational fear brought on by clear and present danger. Recall the single mother and photographer from chapter 3. It's terrifying to be a single parent and not know how on earth you're going to put food in front of your child tonight or pay next month's rent. She had every right to be fearful. (My mom's day-to-day struggle to feed us and keep a roof over our heads is another example.)

Then there are those things that frighten us because they represent merely imagined threats. "If I develop my photography portfolio and start showing it to agencies, they might laugh at me." Those kinds of fears are ones we create in our own minds: fear of failure, fear of social embarrassment. They are very different from the rational, objective concern that there's not enough money to make next month's rent.

My friend Kurt was terrified of flying. Millions of Americans know this fear on some level. This was a crushing problem for him, as his business as a software salesman required that he fly to make pitches in corporate offices in cities all over the country. Every time he had a scheduled flight, he'd start worrying about it days in advance, working himself into a panic by the day of the actual flight. He'd huddle in his seat on the plane, terrified at every bump of turbulence, every noise. Kurt knew that his fear was not a rational one. He was aware that although dying in a fiery plane crash is one of the most horrible deaths we can imagine, for the vast majority of us *imagining* it is all we'll ever do; statistically speaking, you're far safer on a transatlantic flight than you are in your own bathroom.

But this kind of irrational fear isn't easily overcome by applying reason and statistics. It's an associative fear, a fear of the imagination, and in a real sense these kinds of fears and phobias can be much harder to deal with than fear of a real and present danger. Real danger eventually goes away—you can run away from the snarling pit bull. It's harder to run away from the Black Dog in your mind. A phobia forms an endless loop in your imagination. This man associated flying with his fear of flying—every time he thought about flying, it invoked fear. It's a vicious, self-reinforcing cycle: You begin to fear your fears.

Kurt forced himself to fly, because maintaining a successful business outweighed for him (if just barely) his fears. But many of us let our phobias—fear of public speaking, fear of meeting strangers, fear of trying anything new, and so on—defeat us.

Earlier I discussed how fear of failure causes people to "choke" in moments of stress, or prevents them from even trying to improve their lives at all. Ironically, there's another kind of fear that holds people back: *fear of success.*

It sounds strange, but it's true—and if you examine your own life, you may find examples when you, too, decided not to strive for something because you feared the consequences of achieving it. Maybe you think that you're unworthy of success and the recognition it might bring. You lack confidence in your ability not only to achieve, but then to maintain success. You fear that if you abandon your cubicle in the marketing department at Xerox and open your own boutique advertising agency, the friends you made at Xerox will envy and hate you. Or you worry that you might not have what it takes to run your own agency, and will find a way of alienating your largest client and self-destructing.

Fear of success can be just as debilitating as fear of failure. It can prevent you from striving to improve your life. It can become a self-fulfilling prophecy, motivating you to self-destructive behavior that trips you up just when you've decided to quit your job as an office manager, sign up for the weekly open mike at the Funnybone Factory, and do what it takes to become a comedian. You may convince yourself that you'd rather stay where you are in life and resign yourself to quiet, familiar failure than accomplish your goals and then risk losing what you've achieved and acquired. If you get trapped in this kind of mind-set, you may even cause yourself to screw up the ad campaign for that big client just to prove to yourself that you were right all along in your low self-esteem, pessimism, and negativity. "I'm nothing special. I have no right to think I can be a success. I'm not worthy of happiness. Even if I achieve happiness, I'll only screw it all up, and then I'll be worse off than I am now."

Like phobias, these feelings of pessimism and negativity can be self-reinforcing. The more you're convinced that the world is a terrible place and you're a loser who doesn't deserve even to try for happiness, the easier it is to resign yourself to your "fate" and avoid attempting to better your lot. And if you do try, the first setback or obstacle can convince you that you were right to be pessimistic all along. "See? I *knew* I was a loser! What made me think I could ever accomplish anything?"

As with phobias, **the key here is learning how to break those mental habits and stop the behavioral loops that reinforce negativity.** Instead of resigning yourself to failure, you need to learn to be more accepting of yourself and *allow* yourself to achieve and enjoy the fruits of your achievement. You *can* achieve happiness, and you *do* deserve it—every human being deserves to live a life that's as happy and fulfilled as possible. Know this, understand this, believe this, and stop creating obstacles to your own happiness. Success is hard enough to achieve, and your path will be filled with enough challenges. You don't need to make extra ones.

Mao Tse-tung, who led the Chinese Communists from a peasant uprising to a superpower, said, "The longest journey begins with the first step." Taking life one step at a time is one formula for conquering fear. If the path to your ultimate goal seems strewn with too many insurmountable objects, so that the whole process becomes too overwhelming even to attempt, then you need to deconstruct those problems, break them down into bits you can handle. It's deconstructing fears, rather than simple denial, that makes them go away. That may mean going into short-term-survival mode and concentrating most of your energy on paying next month's rent—but still leaving a little time and energy left over to devote to planting the seeds that are eventually going to bloom for you.

It's also a very useful psychological tool to **put your fears in their proper context.** You will see that a lot of the things you fear really aren't so terrifying at all. Psychologists call this "framing" your fears. Ask yourself what's the absolute worst that can happen. Try to imagine the worst catastrophe that could befall you as you continue along your path through the woods toward your Grail. And then realize that, short of death, there's really nothing that can prevent you from achieving your goal eventually if you don't let it.

Some fears and phobias can be addressed directly. If you're terrified of public speaking, for instance, there are courses in public speaking you can take that will gradually help you to deal with and work through that fear. If you have a terror of flying, there are specific therapy programs easily available that help you to identify, analyze, and cope with that fear. And so on.

Hemingway stressed the imaginary nature of many of our fears when he wrote that cowardice "is almost always simply a lack of ability to suspend the functioning of the imagination." The main point to remember about these kinds of imaginary fears and phobias—as well as the anxiety and stress that accompany them—is that they are mental habits. They are patterns of behavior that become self-reinforcing over time. The key to many of the available therapy programs for managing these emotions is breaking the habit, and learning to employ simple mental exercises that will help you do that.

Woody Allen once joked that eighty percent of success is simply showing up. That is, **you'll never succeed if you're too scared to even try.** Theodore Roosevelt put it in a more florid way: "The credit belongs to the man who is actually in the arena, whose face is marred by dust and sweat and blood; who strives valiantly; who errs, who comes short again and again, because there is no effort without error and shortcoming; but who does actually strive to do the deeds; who knows great enthusiasms, the great devotions; who spends himself in a worthy cause; who at the best knows in the end the triumph of high achievement, and who at the worst, if he fails, at least fails while daring greatly, so that his place shall never be with those cold and timid souls who neither know victory nor defeat."

To have courage for whatever comes in life—
everything lies in that.
—Mother Teresa

REVIEW

- Everyone knows fear. Everyone doubts his or her talents and vision sometimes. Successful people find a way to get around those doubts and persevere.

- Persistence, courage, faith in yourself, and relentless determination aren't character traits successful people were lucky enough to be born with. They are psychological tools successful people learn to use.

- You cannot eliminate fear. You can only redirect fear. The difference between a hero and a coward isn't that the hero feels no fear. It's that the hero does his duty despite the fear. He learns to control and channel it.

- Learn how to break the mental habits and stop the behavioral loops that reinforce fear and negativity.

- Put your fears in their proper context. You will see that a lot of the things you fear really aren't so terrifying at all.

- Do not let fear hold you back. You'll never succeed if you're too scared to even try.

E X E R C I S E :   What Am I Afraid Of?

Sometimes fear is a rational response to actual danger. Other fears, also known as phobias, are irrational responses to imaginary threats. The list of phobias is as boundless as the human imagination. Some, like claustrophobia, the fear of insects, and the fear of heights, are relatively common. Others are more rare and might strike us as "silly" — unless we happen to share that fear. Some of the stranger-sounding phobias that have been identified include fear of wind (ancraophobia), fear of glass (hyalophobia), fear of beards (pogonophobia), and fear of puppets (pupaphobia).

As this list suggests, what we fear is often not the object or situation itself but memories or emotions we *associate* with it. We often form these negative associations in childhood, and by the time we're adults they've become mental habits that can be hard to break.

The first step to coping with irrational fears and phobias is to identify (a) what you fear, (b) why you fear it, and (c) how you feel and act when confronted with it. For example: (a) I have an irrational fear of dogs. (b) I've been afraid of dogs since my neighbors' Doberman leaped out of that bush and startled me when I was five years old. (c) When I see a dog, even though I can easily see it presents no real danger to me, I feel a need to run away or cross the street to avoid being anywhere near it.

This knowledge won't magically make the fear disappear. It can, however, be the catalyst for learning how to break your habitual responses to what you fear. There are a number of psychological tools and techniques designed to help with this process; you can research them at the library, the bookstore, or online. You may also want to seek professional help in finding the techniques that work best for you. This exercise is intended only as a first step to identifying and analyzing your fears and how you react to them.

1. I have an irrational fear of the following objects or situations (list all that apply):

   A. _____

   B. _____

   C. _____

   D. _____

   E. _____

2. When I think back, the first time I can recall being afraid of each object/situation I listed above was when:

   A. _____

   B. _____

   C. _____

   D. _____

   E. _____

3. When I encounter or even think about encountering each of the objects or situations listed above, I have the following physical reactions (for example, my heart races, my palms sweat, I feel like I will faint, I walk/run the other way):

   A. _____

   B. _____

   C. _____

   D. _____

   E. _____

4. Thinking about my answers to the above, can I identify some underlying reason that I fear or avoid each object/situation I listed? What do I think I gain by continuing to respond to this particular fear or phobia? What do I lose by not learning how to break this habit?

   _____

   _____

   _____

   _____

   _____

5. Thinking about my answers, I can see how some of my irrational fears are more severe than others, and do more to inhibit or prevent me from living a full and happy life. If I were to list my fears in order, from the one I think inhibits me the most to the one that inhibits me the least, they would be:

   A. _____

   B. _____

(continued)

C. _____

D. _____

E. _____

6. Considering my answers to item 5, the irrational fear I think I should begin to deal with *this week* is:

_____

_____

7. My plan for doing that is:

_____

_____

Be Honorable

*Character cannot be developed in ease and quiet.
Only through experience of trial and suffering can
the soul be strengthened, vision cleared, ambition
inspired, and success achieved.*

—HELEN KELLER

JUDGING CHARACTER

*O*thello is one of Shakespeare's greatest, and most tragic, plays. It's about trust and honesty—or rather, a cataclysmic lack of both. Othello is a magnificent warrior, but he has a huge flaw: He doesn't know whom to trust and whom not to. When he passes over one of his subordinates, Iago, for a promotion, Iago plots revenge. He launches an insidious campaign of lies and tricks to undermine Othello's faith in his most trusted lieutenant as well as in his wife, Desdemona. Thoroughly deceitful, Iago convinces Othello that Desdemona has been cheating on him. Othello foolishly believes and trusts Iago, and murders Desdemona in a jealous rage. Then, when Iago's plot is revealed and Othello realizes the magnitude of his mistake, he kills himself.

Othello may be the worst judge of character in dramatic literature. Iago is a clever and persistent liar, but Shakespeare gives Othello several opportunities to stop, think, and realize he's being "played." He never considers what a shallow person Iago is. Iago is submissive and flatters Othello, but speaks of Othello's friends and wife with bitterness, spite, and hatred. It never occurs to Othello that this is not someone he can put his faith in. Instead, he literally puts his life in this man's hands.

Desdemona, meanwhile, is thoroughly faithful, loving, and loyal. She is so obedient to him (obedience in a wife being a mark of extreme virtue in Shakespeare's day) that she doesn't even put up a fight when he strangles her to death—she obediently lies back and allows him to murder her. But even at that moment, Othello still believes Iago's vicious lies about her.

Othello is brave in battle, but he's fatally indecisive when it comes to his personal affairs. He can command armies but has no control over his own insecurities. Off the field of battle, he can't tell his friends from his enemies. He betrays his friends, and the love of his devoted wife, because he distrusts their honesty and believes Iago's lies.

The word *character* comes from the Greek word for "engrave." This is apt, because what we think of as character probably has less to do with qualities you're born with than with modes of thinking and behavior that you acquire in life. In a sense, your character is "engraved" onto you by your environment and your experiences. Qualities like loyalty, honesty, trustworthiness, courage, and compassion are apparently not innate or hard-wired into our nervous systems; they are behavioral patterns one learns and develops—or not—as a human being interacting with the world. Character building ideally begins at home, in the child's relationship with parents, and continues as one ventures out into the world and encounters teachers and other role models.

We also expect parents to give children their first lessons in ethics—rules that distinguish good conduct from bad, like the Golden Rule: "Do unto others as you would have them do unto you." The child whose home and school environments do not teach such values clearly enters the world ethically challenged. Sadly, all societies seem to include many adults whose lack of character and ethics can be traced directly to their upbringing.

But "a poor upbringing" is a terrible excuse for unethical behavior. As an adult, in both your personal and your public life, you constantly come into situations that test your character. When you borrow your neighbor's new Explorer and put a nick in the bumper in the mall parking lot, it might seem easier to say some other driver must have rammed it while you were inside shopping. When you're having a ladies' night out at La Palapa and they start gossiping about Cyndie, whom you like, your loyalty to her is tested; do you speak up for her or just laugh along with the others? You're rushing down a sidewalk and see an elderly man with a walker struggling with the door to his apartment building, and you have to decide whether to help him or pretend you don't notice. Like the other challenges you face in life, each of these events is an opportunity to grow, to learn something about yourself, to make improvements. It's the accumulation of these events in your life that "engraves" your character, for good or ill. You can't blame your parents for your lack of character. **Your character, like everything else in your life, is yours and yours alone to shape.**

Judging character—knowing whom to trust and whom not, being able to distinguish your real friends from false ones—is not an easy skill to develop. There's no science to it, though for thousands of years people have tried to develop one. The ancients thought you could read a person's character in their facial features; it's called physiognomy. Well into the twentieth century, some people even believed in the practice of phrenology: discovering a person's character by feeling the bumps on their head. The practice of astrology, which seeks to delineate a person's character by the stars and planets of their birth date, remains extremely popular. And if you've ever been to Madame Zerinka the palm reader, she most likely spent far less time predicting your future than describing your character as it is supposedly revealed in your hands.

Most of us don't find reading a person's character as easy as reading the lines in their palms. If your vision is an exciting one and you're good at inspiring others to help you realize it, you're going to attract all sorts of people. At first it's hard to know whether a person is joining forces with you because they share your vision, or simply see in you an opportunity they can exploit to their benefit. The latter sort of person is often a good actor and can easily fool you into believing he or she is truly engaged in your goals. It's usually when the group is facing a moment of stress or crisis that these people show their true colors and lack of commitment. In moments of stress, these uncommitted people will be the first ones to desert or betray you.

I saw this phenomenon in my last year at StarMedia, when the company was suddenly facing enormous challenges and betrayal was a daily occurrence. It was an educational, and extremely painful, lesson to see who remained loyal and steadfast under those trying conditions—and who didn't. Certain investors and business partners, who I'd perhaps naively believed shared our vision, were the first ones to run. (As Julius Caesar once said about some cowardly senators, "quite the clutch of hens.") There were a few who were even actively scheming and conspiring against the company, trying to manipulate the situation for their personal financial gain. I admit I was dumbfounded to find that I had inadvertently brought into our circle people who lacked integrity and in the end were driven by personal gain. I learned the hard way how difficult it can be to judge character.

The upside of that situation was how very gratifying it was

that so many other people pulled together at that time of crisis, rallied to support the company, and remained faithful and committed to the vision. For these people, the StarMedia idea transcended the company's stock price.

When someone betrays your friendship and trust, your natural response is to pull into your shell and tell yourself you're never going to trust anyone again. This is the wrong decision. No matter how hurt you've been by betrayal, you cannot stop trusting in others. For everyone who betrays your trust, so many other people will prove to be worthy of your friendship and will enrich your life in many ways. It takes courage to live a full life in this world, and that includes having the courage to expose yourself to the occasional betrayal.

In the end, **the only person you can guarantee will be trustworthy and honest is you.** You can't force other people to act ethically. But by being scrupulously ethical yourself, you will attract good people whom you can trust and who will join you in actualizing your vision. It's very definitely worth risking the occasional heartache.

DEFINING FRIENDSHIP

Because every setback and failure is a learning opportunity, I did spend a lot of time analyzing how I had put myself in the position of trusting people I shouldn't have. How did I allow so many "close" people to betray me? What was it about me that made me so naive?

I realized that one mistake I had made was to project my own character onto others. As I've noted before, creating and building StarMedia was never about personal financial gain for me. I had a vision of connecting all of Latin America via the Internet, and I set out to realize that dream. Making money while doing that was

Tell me who's your friend and I'll tell you who you are.

— RUSSIAN PROVERB

nice, but it was not what drove me. I also found that once I was rich, *having* lots of money didn't particularly interest me either. When I could buy anything in the world, no matter the price, I started to realize how little I really wanted and how small my real needs are. For me, being rich was not an objective but a result.

What I learned, which clearly should have been obvious to me, is that many people one encounters in the business world are in fact motivated only by money. In some cases, their ethical decisions are made according to a kind of a human spreadsheet, where what's "right" is what brings them financial gain.

So that's one important lesson: **Do not project your own ethics and character onto other people.** Do not assume that everyone attracted to you is really buying into your vision. Some of them are simply going to use you and your vision for their own benefit. Especially when you're entering any sort of business relationship with someone, ask yourself: "Is this relationship based on mutual values, mutual affection, and a shared vision? Or is this person entering a relationship with me out of need, because I represent something—opportunity, energy, ideas, whatever it is— that they want to siphon from me? Is this relationship based solely on their self-interest?"

These are good questions to ask, even though the answers may be hard to discern. Don't become paranoid or overly suspicious of others, and don't close yourself off to people who may help you achieve your goals. But don't simply assume that everyone is motivated by the same goals you are. Don't give away your trust too cheaply. As Ronald Reagan advised, advice that I unfortunately ignored, "Trust, but verify."

Another lesson I learned will seem obvious to anyone with business experience, but I had to learn it the hard way: **Don't confuse a business friendship with a personal friendship.** A business relationship may involve or develop into a true personal friendship, but you must never forget that this isn't its primary motivation. You and a partner, a colleague, an investor, an employer, or an employee may find that you really like each other on a personal level, and that's great. But at bottom what brought you together is business and financial gain, as opposed to affection. At times of crisis or stress, the bottom line that decides how your "friend" behaves will likely be money, not affection.

Maintaining in your own mind the distinction between personal and professional relationships is a critical factor in how you react when that "friend" fails you or betrays you. When it became apparent to some of my colleagues that a certain other of my colleagues was actively working against StarMedia, literally working to undermine us for her own personal gain, I was extremely hesitant to believe it. I liked this person very much and, projecting my own character onto her, simply could not conceive of her deceiving us. Even when she demonstrated in almost obvious ways that she was up to no good, I kept making excuses for her. "We must be misinterpreting her actions," I thought. "Surely there's some rational explanation for what she's doing."

There wasn't. This person was betraying us, plain and simple. By the time I reluctantly admitted this to myself, she had done us tremendous damage.

In the end, this act of betrayal was a gift of knowledge and, hopefully, wisdom. If you keep your personal and business relationships separate in your mind, it's much easier to see and admit it when someone you trust starts doing damage to you, and you can move much more quickly to remedy that bad situation. You can assess the situation more objectively and rationally, and respond more actively and decisively, if your thinking is not clouded by your emotional reactions. As disappointed as you may be with that person, and with yourself for having trusted him, you can still act.

No matter how careful you are to keep the personal and the business separate, when a business colleague fails you and you "break up" with them, it can be just as personally painful to you as breaking up with someone you love. In a real sense, when you have an intense business relationship with someone, and you're working very hard together to achieve mutual goals and make something great happen in the world, it is very much like a romantic relationship, and the breakup can be just as devastating to you emotionally. You may be plunged into deep despair and depression over it. You brood over memories of that incredible week the two of you spent every night in the office wolfing down pizza and laughing hysterically over punch-drunk jokes as you slammed together that make-or-break presentation for the Friday-morning client meeting. You lie on the couch listlessly flicking the remote and stumble across a cop show set in Miami, and you suddenly remember the great three days the two of you spent there at that annual conference. Your cell phone is on the nightstand, and you keep checking it compulsively for the message that never comes.

That painful post-relationship stage may last for weeks, or months, or even years. You have to accept it as part of living in the world and engaging with other people. Sometimes it hurts. But as time goes by, you'll gradually integrate the pain into your life's experiences. A key to this is to **accept your own responsibility for what happened.** I don't mean to beat yourself up over it or wallow in guilt. But at some point you need to say to yourself, "I am the author of my own life. I am responsible for what happens to me in this life." And then you can begin to analyze what *you* did that allowed or even caused that person to act the way they did. You admit your mistakes, analyze them, and learn from them.

Finally, it's also crucial to your own mental health and development as a human being to **forgive the person who betrayed you.** As hard as this may be, as terribly as they may have damaged and disappointed you, at some point you have to forgive them. Have pity for them, because in acting the way they did, they damaged themselves a lot more than they damaged you. Betrayal, as the Dalai Lama pointed out, eats at the soul of the betrayer. And for your part, until you can bring yourself to forgive them, some part of you is always going to be stuck in the past, picking the scab, dwelling on the pain they caused you, inhibiting you from moving forward.

It took me time, and much meditation, but I've forgiven those who betrayed me—and have set myself free.

SELF-BETRAYAL

You don't need to go to Shakespeare to read tragic stories of leaders who betray the trust of their followers. You can read similar tales all the time in the business pages of the daily newspapers. Stories of corporate CEOs who lie, cheat, and steal from their employees, stockholders, and investors are common—and follow a sadly familiar pattern. Every year, we read of the trial of some high-flying corporate officer who, though he was legitimately making a salary of millions of dollars, was caught helping himself to millions more by manipulating his company's stock prices, or raiding his employees' pension fund, or lying to his board, or flagrantly abusing the corporate expense account to pay for extraordinary personal extravagances.

Take the CEO who was charged recently for allegedly looting hundreds of millions of corporate funds, which apparently helped finance his string of mansions, his wife's and mistresses' millions of dollars in jewelry, his yacht, and even a $2 million birthday bash. This was a man who *legally* earned $300 million over five years. If the charges are proven true, we must ask why a man earning so much felt the irresistible need to take more—and was willing to risk up to thirty years in jail for it.

Even on Wall Street, where supposedly "greed is good," a leader who's too much out for himself at the expense of others may come to a bad end. The Wall Street institutional crisis sparked by a wave of corporate scandals has led to a profound refocusing on core values. Earning and maintaining trust is now the paramount concern of practically every Wall Street leader.

There's an obvious and simple lesson in such stories—so much so, in fact, that it's astounding how often some people seem to forget or ignore it. Leaders perhaps are able to thrive for a while being untrustworthy and dishonest, but in the end they ensure their own downfall. In any endeavor where you're responsible to other people and they are responsible to you, if you breach that contract or abuse that trust, you *will* in the end pay for it.

You cannot expect others to be trustworthy if you are untrustworthy. You cannot count on others to be honest if you are dishonest. You may make yourself look good to your department head by taking credit for someone else's idea, you may be able to buy yourself an extra beer tonight because you shortchanged that hurried man at your checkout counter, you may be able to get away for months or even years with putting private dinners on the company expense account, but in the long term you're dooming yourself to failure. Because eventually even the most clever liars and cheats are uncovered. They risk losing not only everything they gained in terms of ill-gotten wealth, but also the love, respect, and support of the people they betrayed. Coming back from that abyss could take a lifetime.

The real point is that when you lie or cheat, when you betray the trust of others, *you're betraying yourself and your vision.* You are never going to be truly happy or achieve success as a human being if you build your life on lies. **On the path of life, there are no shortcuts to personal fulfillment.** You may be able to cheat your way to some of the *external trappings* of success—wealth, power, fame—but you can't cheat the process of understanding yourself, the process of finding those paths that are truly appropriate for you and are going to make you happy.

LEADING BY EXAMPLE

Obviously, it's quite possible to become very rich and "successful" in the world while being a completely selfish person who's only out for number one. Such people can even run huge corporations, with lots of people working under them.

But is such a person truly a leader? Do people follow them out of loyalty or a shared vision? Does such a person create anything in the world besides his own personal fortune?

No. True leadership is not about yourself. It's selfless. It transcends you and your own needs. True leadership serves ideas or needs or issues that are bigger than you. And it inspires others to transcend as well. **Real leaders lead by example.**

King Juan Carlos of Spain clearly understands and lives by these principles. He leads his people by his character and his conduct, not through any sort of autocratic power. He has dedicated himself to being the finest person he can be, and to inspiring the people of his country to be the finest people they can be, too. He knows that if he were to act in ways that are unethical, immoral, or inappropriate, he'd be betraying not only his people but himself and his vision for the nation.

That's the attitude of a true leader. A true leader doesn't just boss people around for his own benefit and glory. A true leader devotes himself to a higher cause and inspires others through his example to devote their lives to this greater cause as well.

You don't have to be a king to show that kind of leadership. A great teacher, for example, inspires students to be the best they can be, and in so doing enriches not only the community but the life of each of those students.

Edwin Correa left Puerto Rico at the age of sixteen, bent on a career that makes heroes in both Latin and North America: He became a major-league pitcher. Then, after retiring from a fine career with the Texas Rangers in the late 1980s, he began a second career—one that, in my opinion, makes him a real hero. He returned to Puerto Rico and founded the Puerto Rico Baseball Academy High School. The Academy prepares talented young ballplayers for a potential career in the sport, but its goal is much higher than that. Correa, who never attended college himself, stresses academic success as well as athletics. He seeks to inspire and help young Puerto Ricans to become well-rounded individuals—not just the best ballplayers they can be, but the best people.

Whatever you do, you can always find opportunities to transcend and become a leader through your inspiration and example. By being the best person you can be—honest, trustworthy, responsible, courteous, and ethical—you inspire such qualities in those around you. By devoting yourself to a higher goal, you inspire others to expect more of themselves as well.

And *that's* true success, regardless of whether it brings you those external trappings.

REVIEW

- Your character, like everything else in your life, is yours and yours alone to shape.

- In your dealings with others, the only person you can guarantee will be trustworthy and honest is you yourself. Do not project your own ethics and character onto other people.

- Don't confuse a professional friendship for personal friendship. Maintaining in your mind the distinction between personal and business relationships is a critical factor in how you react when a "friend" fails you or betrays you.

- If a friend has betrayed you, accept your own responsibility for what happened. Admit your mistakes, analyze them, and learn from them.

- It's crucial to your mental health and development as a human being to forgive the person who betrays you. Free yourself through forgiveness.

- On the path of life, there are no shortcuts to personal fulfillment. You cannot expect others to be trustworthy if you are untrustworthy. You cannot count on others to be honest if you are dishonest.

- Real leaders lead by example. Whatever you do, you can always find opportunities to transcend and become a leader through your inspiration and example.

E X E R C I S E : Choosing Friends

We choose friends for complex reasons. There can be many reasons we are attracted to people and want to be friends with them. Good, lasting friendships enrich and enlarge our lives. Poorly chosen friends can be extremely destructive to us.

It is difficult to tell in advance if someone you like and want to be friends with is going to have a positive or a negative impact on your life. But looking back, you may be able to see patterns in how you've chosen friends that distinguish the good friendships from the bad ones. Knowing how you've chosen friends in the past may help you make more positive choices and avoid the wrong kinds of friends in the future.

This exercise is intended to help you start that process of analysis.

1. The friends who have most helped me in my life are (list as many as apply):
   A. _____
   B. _____
   C. _____
   D. _____
   E. _____

2. Looking back, I think that the qualities, characteristics, or personality traits that attracted me to each of these people were:
   A. _____
   B. _____
   C. _____
   D. _____
   E. _____

3. The friends who have been most destructive to me in my life are (list as many as apply):
   A. _____
   B. _____
   C. _____
   D. _____
   E. _____

4. The qualities, characteristics, or personality traits that attracted me to each of these people were:

A. _____

B. _____

C. _____

D. _____

E. _____

5. What qualities, characteristics, or personality traits do the first group of friends and the second have in common?

_____

_____

6. What qualities, characteristics, or personality traits distinguish the first group from the second?

_____

_____

7. What does this tell me about what attracts me to people and how I choose friends? About what kinds of people are most likely to be good friends to me? About what kinds of people are most likely to be destructive to me?

_____

_____

8. The last time a person I thought was a friend betrayed me was (write a brief description of what happened):

_____

_____

_____

_____

_____

(continued)

9. In retrospect, were there warning signs that this person might betray me? If so, they were:

_____

_____

10. How did I respond to these signs? Did I ignore them, deny them, refuse to believe them? Did I investigate them? Did I speak to my friend about them?

_____

_____

_____

_____

_____

11. Did I act decisively to limit the negative impact of this person's betrayal, or was I more passive in allowing myself to be hurt by it? Why?

_____

_____

_____

_____

_____

12. What can I learn about myself, and about how I choose friends, from this experience? How can I use what this experience teaches me about myself when choosing friends in the future?

_____

_____

_____

_____

_____

Integrate Body, Mind, and Spirit

*T*he Latin poet Juvenal declared that the ideal Roman citizen possessed *mens sana in corpore sano*—a sound mind in a sound body. I would add a third dimension to be integrated in the ideal person: a sound mind and a sound spirit in a sound body.

INTEGRATING MIND AND BODY

For centuries, Western medicine and Western culture in general treated the mind, the spirit, and the body as separate and unrelated entities. The body was thought of as little more than a temporary vehicle that carried the mind and the soul around this earth. Indeed, because Christianity saw the body as a source of temptation and sin, physical existence was denigrated and downplayed, while mental and spiritual life were treated as innately superior to and "purer" than the physical.

Only fairly recently has the West come to understand how closely the body and mind are integrated and interrelated. We know now that our mental and emotional states can have a direct effect on our physical health, and that in turn there's a physiological basis for many of our mental and emotional states. So, on the one hand, chronic depression seems to inhibit the body's resistance to disease; on the other, imbalances in brain chemistry cause symptoms of mental illness.

The relationship of stress to heart disease and other illnesses is now well accepted by the medical community. Stress was first identified in the 1930s, though it remains difficult to pin a precise definition on it. Like fear, stress seems to tap into our primordial fight-or-flight instincts; but where fear is an immediate burst of response to danger (real or imagined), stress is apparently a more constant condition—and therefore may have a prolonged negative effect on health. It's as though the mind and the body are in a continual state of low-level fear, with no respite, none of the relaxation and release of tension that we usually enjoy when a specific danger has passed. The link between stress and heart disease has been well documented, but stress is also thought to have a much more widespread impact on the body, affecting the nervous, respiratory, and immune systems, causing sleep and eating disorders, reducing memory and concentration, and triggering certain mental and emotional disorders.

Job-related stress is a well-known phenomenon. It can strike the overachieving corporate manager, the overworked air-traffic controller, and the politician under constant public scrutiny. A home that's racked by constant conflict, violence, or abuse puts children under terrible stress. It's now thought that the daily pressures of living in impoverished urban neighborhoods produce a level of stress that is a contributing factor in the disturbing cluster of increased health risks faced by poor people.

We're beginning to understand other ways that the mind and the body are related. For example, the IQ test, which has been used for roughly a century to measure intelligence, probes only for linguistic, mathematical, and logical skills—what we might call "brain intelligence." But in recent decades, education scholars like Harvard's Howard Gardner have argued that this is a limiting and misleading way of judging intelligence. Gardner theorizes "multiple intelligences"—different forms of intelligence that we all possess in varying levels. These include the "body intelligence" best seen in athletes, dancers, and people good with their hands; the visual-spatial intelligence demonstrated by artists; and the interpersonal intelligence that translates into good social skills.

This theory makes intuitive sense. When we watch an athlete perform with extreme skill, we often say he or she played "brilliantly." We don't mean that he or she would necessarily score high on the IQ test. We mean that they're demonstrating a physical genius, an intelligence of the body that's just as impressive and real as the intelligence of a math whiz.

Dancers, obviously, also exhibit body intelligence. Merce Cunningham is one of the most innovative choreographers in modern dance. His approach is as spiritual and philosophical as it is artistic. Borrowing from such sources as Zen Buddhism, the I Ching, and theoretical physics, he's especially known for experimenting with chance and random occurrence. He deconstructs the traditional dance concert into basic elements: movement, gesture, bodies moving through time and space, music, lights, set. Then he lets chance determine the sequence and arrangement of these elements. Although the elements remain constant, the way they are presented could change with every performance.

The impact on his dancers is profound and revelatory. Since no concert is ever routine, no dancer can ever go on "autopilot." The randomness factor means that they have to be fully "in the moment" every second they are on stage, completely attuned to their own bodies, to all the other dancers, and to all the other elements of the performance. Although every movement is precise and rigorously rehearsed, the ever-shifting context makes each performance a new creative act, not a repetition. It requires an extraordinary integration of their bodies, their minds, and, I would argue, their spirits.

Americans have reached a curious and fascinating crossroads

in how they regard and respect their bodies. As I noted earlier, more Americans are obese now than ever before. It is the fastest-growing cause of disease and death in the country. But at the same time, millions of other Americans have been on a prolonged "health kick" for the last thirty years. We jog, run, bike, or walk for our cardiovascular health. We go to gyms and exercise classes in ever-increasing numbers. We've raised concerns about a healthy diet to the level of a national obsession. Simultaneously, Americans are in the best physical shape they've ever been, and the worst.

We know that there are factors of class, economics, and culture that promote obesity in some sectors of society. In certain Latin American cultures, a body that some of us would call overweight is seen as a sign of success in males (he must be successful if he can afford to eat so much) and sexually attractive in females. (I have a female Cuban friend whose parents agonized about her trim, athletic figure throughout her youth. They nicknamed her "Flaca"—Skinny—and they didn't mean it as a compliment.) In many impoverished areas, both urban and rural, poor people have little or no access to healthy foods or gymnasiums, so that a bad diet and lack of exercise are almost conditions of their social environment.

Even granting these factors, however, I believe that the national obesity epidemic signals a deeper hunger. Like other addictive behaviors, compulsive eating is a distorted attempt to achieve a false and fleeting sense of happiness.

But **you'll never achieve true happiness by abusing your body** that way. You can't climb mountains if you're eating compulsively. You can't follow your path to success if you stop in every fast-food joint along the route.

My own overeating when I was a boy was clearly an attempt to achieve some comfort and happiness under extremely trying and stressful conditions. But rather than bring me happiness, it triggered some very negative effects on my health and morale. I developed high blood pressure and would be sent home from school with dizzy spells. I had a terribly negative self-image.

I finally shed the extra weight in college, losing fifty-five pounds in one semester. But I didn't begin to exercise regularly until I was in my late twenties. I experimented with exercises and settled on hiking as the one best suited to me. (Nepal was a test of my new focus on hiking.)

Within six months I could see and feel the positive changes—not just in my body but in my mind as well. Up until then, I had pretty much believed that old-fashioned model of the body as just a vehicle for carrying my brain around. I suppose I was the classic "pencil-necked geek." Now I discovered for myself the intimate relationship between the body's health and the mind's capabilities. The act of getting into shape and following a good diet vastly increased my levels of mental as well as physical energy and stamina. I could think more clearly and concentrate more sharply. I found that when I went on my daily hike I was taking not just my body out for exercise, but my mind, too. After all, the blood and oxygen that pumps through your body when you exert it also feeds your brain. When I hike, my mind becomes clear and focused. I've had some of my most creative ideas while hiking. My work schedule permitting, I try to hike nearly every day.

There are other ways that physical, mental, and emotional health interact and reinforce one another. The term "biofeedback" may be a New Age cliché, but it describes processes that are quite real and have become well-known to the scientific and medical communities. Many hospitals and clinics now acknowledge the correlation between a positive, optimistic attitude and the body's ability to heal injury, recover from radical surgery, or fight off disease. We know from our own lives the way that anxiety can give us a sleepless night, which produces both physical and mental exhaustion. Or the way a long bout of depression brings on not only physical lethargy and neglect but an inability to focus our minds and think clearly.

I have learned a few simple techniques for bringing my body, mind, and emotions in synch. One is a yoga like controlled-breathing exercise. Focusing intently on a process of deep, regular breathing has a remarkable calming effect on my emotions in times of stress or worry, which in turn frees my mind to focus sharply on whatever it is that's worrying me and find a creative solution. I have also discovered the benefits of massage therapy and acupuncture. Our body literally stores tension and stress in our muscles; this muscle tension, in turn, sends constant signals to our brain that keep our mind in a state of agitation. It's a self-reinforcing loop. Massage relaxes the muscles, which allows the mind to relax as well. And acupuncture, a discipline that has been used for thousands of years, is a powerful tool for stress management.

I have proven to myself that **there is a direct, immediate link between physical health, the ability to think creatively, and the emotional stability to persevere.** Getting your mind, your emotions, and your body in balance and harmony is key to your daily pursuit of happiness and fulfillment. It allows you to think about your needs clearly and to plan creatively. It gives you the flexibility to pursue your goals through life's branching pathways, the emotional stamina to persevere, the agility to overcome obstacles along your way, and the resilience to recover and move on when the occasional seven-ton piano falls on your head.

Just as you should keep your body healthy and fit, you must also keep exercising your mind. **The successful person understands that every day brings opportunities for the mind to learn and grow, and takes full advantage of that.** It can be as simple as reading a book like Stephen Hawking's *The Universe in a Nutshell* or the current issue of *The New Republic.* Or watching PBS and the History Channel some nights instead of the usual sitcoms and sports. Or going to the Wednesday-night lecture series at Bookends Café, where you might encounter people with ideas, experiences, and points of view that are new to you. Or traveling to countries you've never visited, where you'll experience other cultures and ways of living. Or it can be a more formal exercise in learning, such as taking that Tuesday-night continuing education class in modern Western philosophy that will challenge your mind with new information or a new perspective.

The learning and growing process is lifelong. Remember my wife's grandmother, learning to play the violin and use a computer in her eighties. You will never know "everything you need to know" about the world or yourself. The greatest geniuses acknowledge that what they know is a tiny fragment of what the world offers. The best and brightest minds, like Hawking and Einstein, never lose their thirst for new knowledge, never lose the excitement of stretching and challenging themselves intellectually.

THE HUMAN SPIRIT

Even if one is not a member of a specific religion, most of us acknowledge that **there's a spiritual dimension to life along with the physical and mental.** Specific definitions of what we mean by spiritual life vary across religions, philosophies, cultures, even from person to person. Yet if you look across all cultures and religions, as Joseph Campbell spent his life doing, you find a striking convergence in the qualities people cite as representing the very best and finest attributes of the human spirit. Many call them virtues. To me, the key qualities include the capacities for love, compassion, charity, self-sacrifice, service to others, justice, courage, and hope. Different philosophies and religions might add to my list, but I doubt if they'd subtract from it.

Unfortunately, while our current society theoretically acknowledges all the best qualities of the human spirit, in practice it tends to measure what makes a successful human being narrowly and disastrously on the false markers of money, power, and fame. Corporate American culture has made much of the "Type A" personality, those obsessives who are so driven to succeed in worldly terms that they'll sacrifice everything human about themselves—including their health and spiritual well-being—to achieve power and wealth. But that's all they achieve. If they ignore the spiritual dimension of life they're not going to be truly happy, and they won't really be successful human beings.

What is the real purpose of life? Is it to make a billion dollars? Or is making a billion dollars one of the possible results of a life well-led? I am not arguing against people making a lot of money. But if your life choices are driven only by a desire to make money, in the end you'll find it to be a hollow victory that might even consume you.

There's a Wall Street billionaire who made his fortune as a corporate raider—or maybe corporate rapist is a more apt term. He bought up some companies only to dismantle them and sell the assets, and inflated the stock values of others only to cash out and leave the other stockholders saddled with debt. This man was able to carve out a fortune through destruction, not by creating anything of value in the world. And in the process he ruined the livelihoods of thousands of people.

Meanwhile, in the hope of salvaging some of his reputation and maybe his soul as well, he became a well-publicized philanthropist, giving huge sums of money away to a variety of causes. Yet no amount of philanthropic giving can alter the fact that he made his fortune through destroying lives.

The term for this is "false charity." It's charity for show, not out of any actual compassion or sense of obligation to do good in the community. In his daily business activities, this corporate rapist demonstrated beyond the shadow of a doubt that he had no compassion.

Many of the world's great philosophers and religious leaders have warned us about false charity. In the Bible, Jesus says, "Take heed that you do not give alms before men, to be seen of them: otherwise you have no reward from your Father in heaven. Therefore, when you give alms, do not sound a trumpet before you, as the hypocrites do in the synagogues and in the streets, that they may have glory of men. Verily I say to you, they have their reward. But when you give alms, let not your left hand know what your right hand is doing, so that your alms may be in secret, and your Father who sees in secret himself shall reward you openly."

False charity is the antithesis of real compassion. Measuring your life's success by how much money you pile up, regardless of the misery and destruction you cause other people in the process, shows a complete lack of the capacity to love or serve others.

And it doesn't matter whether you become a billionaire or just pull down a middle-class salary: If the money you make and the things it buys you are all that motivate you, you're risking spiritual death. Remember Jacob Marley's woeful ghost in Dickens's *A Christmas Carol*, doomed to drag chains of his own making through the gloom of the afterlife. Trying to cheer up his old colleague, Scrooge says to him, "But you were always a good man of business, Jacob." Marley cries, "Business! Mankind was my business. The common welfare was my business; charity, mercy, forbearance, and benevolence, were, all, my business. The dealings of my trade were but a drop of water in the comprehensive ocean of my business!"

Marley is offering his old friend a message of enormous significance. **If you deny the human spirit in yourself, if you fail to feel and act on compassion and love for others, you're not only wronging them but damaging yourself as a human being.**

Just as with intellectual and physical health, spiritual health is crucial to your ability to achieve happiness and success as a human being. It's as self-defeating to let your spiritual side atrophy and die through neglect as it is to abuse your body or stop growing intellectually. To put it another way, *it's in your own self-interest to take an active interest in others.*

Like the body and the mind, the spiritual dimension of life needs "exercise." Even that corporate raider seems to know, intuitively, that doing good in the world is something he "should" aspire to. But it's not enough to know it—you have to *act* on it. Fortunately, the world presents us with innumerable opportunities every day to actively show love, compassion, charity, and kindness. You hold the elevator door for the harried young mother whose son is dragging his feet down the hall. The gaggle of Japanese students in their brand-new hip-hop gear asks you how to get to the crosstown express bus stop. Your church's soup kitchen opens its doors to the homeless every day from four to seven P.M. The receptionist is organizing an office team for next Sunday's 10K AIDS Walk.

You don't need to believe in heaven or karma or Marley's ghost to realize that every time you show compassion or kindness to others, you're doing yourself a favor as well. In actual, practical terms, you enrich and improve your own life when you reach out to others. You can even think of it in a fairly selfish way. Your ability to relate to people is critical to your own process of growth and maturity, of understanding yourself, of healing yourself. Also, if you deal respectfully and kindly with others, you're increasing the chances that they'll do the same with you, which can obviously help you in attaining your goals. At the very, *very* least, it simply makes you feel good about yourself and helps you tap into the optimism and self-esteem that are critical to your own happiness and success.

Ultimately, if you owe it to yourself and to your community

to strive for being the finest person you can be, then you have an obligation to be a *whole* person. The whole person integrates physical, mental, and spiritual health. Integration means growing and maturing in all those dimensions of your life. You will never achieve true success or happiness if you ignore or starve any of those aspects of your humanity.

REVIEW

- The successful human being integrates physical, mental, and spiritual health.

- You'll never achieve true happiness by abusing your body. There is a direct, immediate link between physical health, the ability to think creatively, and the emotional stability to persevere. Getting your mind, your emotions, and your body in balance and harmony is key to your daily pursuit of happiness and fulfillment.

- The successful person understands that every day brings opportunities for the mind to learn and grow, and takes full advantage of that.

- If you deny the human spirit in yourself, if you fail to feel and act on compassion and love for others, you're not only wronging them but damaging yourself as a human being. It's in your own self-interest to take an active interest in others.

E X E R C I S E : Mens Sana in Corpore Sano
(A Sound Mind in a Sound Body)

How well do you take care of yourself physically? How much intellectual "exercise" do you get? Answering the questions below can help you identify aspects of your physical and intellectual well-being that could use some improvement.

Answer True or False to questions 1 through 15.

1. I am in good physical shape.

2. I exercise regularly.

3. I eat a healthy, balanced diet.

4. I smoke.

5. I drink too much coffee.

6. I drink too much alcohol.

7. I drink too much soda.

8. I get regular sleep.

9. I get a regular physical checkup.

10. I get a regular dental checkup.

11. I find it easy to focus my mind and concentrate on a task.

12. Left to my own devices, I tend to daydream and dawdle.

13. I tend to spend my free time in physically or intellectually challenging activities.

14. I tend to spend my free time "vegetating" in front of the TV or just hanging out.

15. I like to learn new things, and I go out of my way to make the opportunity in my life to do that.

(continued)

16. The interests, skills, and/or hobbies I pursue in my free time are (list):

_____

_____

17. I read _____ books in an average month.

18. I read _____ magazines in an average month.

19. I read _____ newspapers in an average week.

20. In the past two years, I've attended _____ course(s)/class(es).

21. In the past two years, I've acquired the following new skills or knowledge:

_____

_____

_____

_____

_____

Do Your Duty to the Community

> To put the world in order, we must first put the
> nation in order; to put the nation in order, we
> must first put the family in order; to put the family
> in order, we must first cultivate our personal life;
> we must first set our hearts right.
>
> — CONFUCIUS

*H*oward Hughes is remembered as one of the wealthiest, most famous, and most successful entrepreneurs of the last century. He is also remembered as one of the loneliest and most unhappy. As a boy growing up in Texas, the son of a "wildcat" oilman, he was a loner who amused himself by tinkering with engines and machines. As a young man, he built his first fortune in oil, then went on to make billions in aeronautics (he owned both Hughes Aircraft and TWA), electronics, and movies (he owned RKO Pictures), and through buying up Las Vegas hotels and casinos like so many Monopoly properties. He was a record-breaking test pilot, and he squired gorgeous movie starlets, from Jean Harlow to Jane Russell to Jean Peters.

And he remained a lonely outsider through it all. At first he tried to buy friends and companionship the way he bought real estate; later he didn't even try. In the last twenty years of his life he became notoriously reclusive and paranoid. He was convinced he was the target of evil conspiracies. The once reckless test pilot grew so terrified of disease that he hid in a self-made antiseptic cell, a "germ-free zone," whiling away his drug-addled final years watching movies and refusing any human contact except with one or two of his most trusted—and presumably cleanest—employees. He died alone, with no friends or family. Because he left no heirs, his vast empire was squabbled over by an ugly cabal of employees, relatives, and rank impostors.

What a lonely, ignominious way for such a wealthy and powerful man to live and die.

Those who are so driven to succeed that they'll sacrifice their friendships and their family life to achieve their goals are misguided and will never know true happiness. Your personal relationships are integral to your humanity and your happiness. These relationships will also help you on your path to success. Family and friends give you support in times of weakness. That healthy support reinforces your energy and perseverance. They also question your decisions and offer honest criticisms, helping you to refine your ideas and focus your energies.

Compare Hughes's life and work to that of another extremely wealthy man, John D. Rockefeller. The man chiefly responsible for the enormous Rockefeller family fortune was every inch a businessman and entrepreneur, and clearly driven to succeed. But he never lost his connections to his family or his community, and never forgot that with great wealth comes the moral responsibility to do great things.

John D. Rockefeller was the creative force that led Standard Oil to dominate the fossil-fuel industry in the second half of the 1800s. He believed that by creating a monopoly in the production and supply of kerosene, which was used to light homes, businesses, and streets throughout the country, he was transforming society for the better.

He carried on in this same spirit as an extraordinarily gifted and dedicated philanthropist. In his lifetime he donated more than half a billion dollars to charity—at the time, a truly colossal fortune. Just as important, he established institutions and foundations that continue to give back to the community long after his death. Institutions that owe their existence to him in whole or in large part include Rockefeller University, the University of Chicago, the Rockefeller Foundation, and the 4-H Clubs. That's just a fragment of his lasting impact in the fields of education, health, the sciences, and social welfare. (His grandson David Rockefeller, an early investor in StarMedia, has continued the family tradition, making a tremendously positive impact with his philanthropy in the United State and the world.)

John D. Rockefeller was a devoted church member and family man, who passed on his dedication for community service to his children and their children. For them, as for him, it seems that wealth and success have little value unless they can be put to productive use for the benefit of all.

Remember the story of Yolanda and Rogelio Garcia in Los Angeles. They live in extreme poverty, but I would argue they're every bit as successful as any Rockefeller—and a lot happier than a Howard Hughes. Their family is the center of their lives, the source of their incredible strength of will and indomitable spirit. The love that binds Rogelio, Yolanda and their children has given them all the power to overcome the massive obstacles in their path and achieve great things. Yolanda and Rogelio may work as "trash pickers" and "dumpster divers," but their lives are enriched beyond measure, and they are true heroes.

The stage and movie star John Leguizamo is another Latin hero. Born in Colombia, he emigrated to the United States with his family and grew up a poor "spic" kid on the streets of Queens, the borough of New York City that has a greater diversity of new immigrant populations than any other place on earth. As a boy he weathered the racist attacks of other kids in the neighborhood, as well as his parents' explosive divorce. He seems only partly joking when he says he developed his flair for comedy as an adolescent's "survival strategy," when a good laugh was the only escape from the stress of daily life.

As a struggling young film and TV actor, Leguizamo had to contend with the ethnic stereotyping that effectively restricted Latin performers to playing *Miami Vice*–style gangsters and drug dealers. He gritted his teeth and took some of those roles (on *Miami Vice* itself, and in films like *Regarding Henry* and *Carlito's Way*), and performed brilliantly in them, often ad-libbing to add human dimension to the characters. Meanwhile, he was writing and starring in his own one-man plays, like *Mambo Mouth* and *Spic-O-Rama*, destroying stereotypes in shows that were humorous, wise, and touching evocations of the lives and families of Latins in the United States.

By the age of forty, Leguizamo had become one of the most successful Latin actors in the world. He makes millions of dollars for appearing in a single Hollywood hit like *Moulin Rouge* or *Ice Age,* but has remained the antithesis of the Hollywood movie star, continuing to live and raise his family in New York City, far from the glitter and hype of Hollywood. And for every Hollywood blockbuster he's starred in, he has written, produced, invested in, directed, and/or starred in a smaller, more realistic film like *Empire* or the HBO hit *Undefeated*, always focusing on depicting Latins with a depth and sensitivity rare in movies. He has never forgotten who he is or where he came from, has remained devoted to the family in which he grew up (his mother is his bookkeeper and financial adviser) and the family he's now raising, and has provided all Latins in this country with a hero and a role model.

In one of their songs, the rock group Jefferson Airplane once quipped, "No man is an island. He's a peninsula!" That's a funny play on the old saying, but it also happens to be a pretty wise observation. Except for a few religious hermits and a handful of hardy souls in the wilderness, none of us lives like an island, in perfect isolation from others. Most of us are more like peninsulas, each responsible for his own life, yet firmly connected to others.

COOPERATION IS CIVILIZATION

The ability to cooperate, to work together to achieve much more than any individual could on his own, was a critical factor in the survival and development of the human species. Our primate cousins—orangutans, chimpanzees, and gorillas—tend to live in loose-knit social groups where fierce competition, for everything from food to sex to status, is the norm. Generally, cooperative behavior seems to be limited to related females (sisters will collaborate on food-gathering and infant care) and, of course, to mothers and their offspring (at least until the young ape is mature enough to fend for and compete for itself).

Around three million years ago, our hominid ancestors began to organize themselves along another social model, one that we would recognize as more "human." They learned to cooperate with one another. Anthropologists suggest that it was the inclusion of meat in their diet that spurred this behavior. Hominids spent a tremendous amount of their time foraging for edible plants, roots, berries, and so on. When they could, they supplemented this vegetarian diet with meat, which provided a feast of proteins and calories not easily obtained from plants. For this reason they've been called hunter-gatherers, although some anthro-

A hundred times every day I remind myself that my inner and outer life depend on the labors of other men, living and dead, and that I must exert myself in order to give in the same measure as I have received and am still receiving.

—ALBERT EINSTEIN

pologists say the more correct term would be gatherer-hunters, since they expended far more time and energy in foraging than in hunting.

Hunting wild animals was a tremendously risky proposition. The lone hunter often came home empty-handed—and hungry. They learned that hunting in groups upped the chances of success. When a successful hunting party returned home, all shared the meat. Thus, everyone in the group benefited from this cooperative behavior, from working together for a shared goal that the individual would not have been able to achieve.

The development of this group behavior was a social revolution. Hunting in groups was the antithesis of gathering and foraging for roots and berries, an intensely solitary chore. We can see this in apes, as each chimp or gorilla ranges through the forest alone, plucking leaves and berries and popping them into its mouth. It's not a system that promotes collaboration or sharing. Reorganizing hominid society along more cooperative lines represented the dawn, or at least the predawn, of civilization.

Hominids gradually evolved into humans, who share not only food and labor but ideas, knowledge, and dreams. No longer hunter-gatherers, we settled in agrarian communities and cities, where cooperative behavior was imperative. Working together, we have achieved feats far beyond the capacity of any single person. Stonehenge (2700–2000 B.C.), the Great Pyramid in Egypt (2500 B.C.), the Great Wall of China (third century B.C.), and the Mayan temples (200–900 A.D.) continue to astound us not only for the engineering genius they display but as massive public-works projects that coordinated the efforts of thousands. In the modern era, projects like the Panama Canal, the Hoover Dam, and the NASA space program are also monuments to humans' collaborative prowess.

Of course, the same could be said of humans working together for evil purposes like genocidal warfare. But even in those tragic instances, the point remains valid: Working in groups, we can far transcend the capabilities of any individual—for good or evil.

THE PERSONAL SUPPORT GROUP

The power of the group is evident on a much more personal scale as well. It's safe to say that **no one who has been truly successful and happy in life has done it alone.** Dean Karnazes, the ultra-endurance athlete, doesn't run his 200-mile races by himself. His wife, children, and parents are his "team." They pace him in a van along the course of his races, providing food and water and, probably most important, love and encouragement. When Lou Gehrig's disease robbed Stephen J. Hawking of the power of speech, his family and friends helped him continue to communicate his genius to the world, one letter at a time. It's not just for the photo op that winning politicians always invite their spouses and families up on stage to celebrate with them. They're well aware that the support and sacrifices of their loved ones were critical to their success.

It is the friends you can call at four A.M. who matter.

—MARLENE DIETRICH

People define their personal support groups in different ways. For some it's the nuclear family; for those of us who are Latin, it's more likely a much-extended family, with many cousins, aunts, uncles, in-laws, and other relatives. Some identify less with the family they were born into than with a network of close friendships they've developed. Others see their neighborhood or their local community as their "family," or perhaps their "tribe."

However you define it, that group nurtures you, encourages you to be your best, and helps you achieve your goals. In times of need or crisis, they depend on you and you on them. These are the people who sustain you, who drive you forward, who help you see things you might not have seen on your own.

I'm thirty-seven years old as I write this, and have been with my wife Ann for seventeen years. I seriously doubt I could have achieved what I have, not to mention surviving the occasional seven-ton piano, without her love and support. I hope that I can say I've been as supportive and nurturing of her, and of our son.

As we all know, you don't get to choose the family you're born into. Children do sometimes break their parents' hearts. Parents sometimes fail miserably to live up to their responsibilities to their children. In my case, as I described briefly in the introduction, my father betrayed my mother and me. His psychological cruelty to her was so severe that she felt the only way to escape it was to leave Uruguay and take me with her (which she did without his assent).

As an eight-year-old boy, there was nothing I could do to prevent him from mistreating her the way he did. Sometimes you can't stop those close to you from doing the wrong thing. But I did learn from that experience, and my relationship with my own son is, I believe, much stronger and loving for my having been subjected to my father's negative example.

Like my marriage, all my best and most dependable friendships are long-term relationships. We've been through a lot together; our friendships have been tested, proven, and refined by life.

But we can also create bad relationships for ourselves in choosing friends. We may look for people who are wrong for us, or for friendships that fill some neurotic need or weakness in us rather than complement our strengths. We may seek friendships that create dependencies or codependencies, as when a weak person with low self-esteem chooses a bullying, abusive mate; or there's the young man who's afraid to study for his GED and try for a more satisfying job than driving a forklift at the warehouse, so he spends all his after-work time hanging out drinking beer with his unambitious pals on the corner. It's easy—and lazy—to associate with people who we believe accept us for what we are, when what they're really doing is failing us as friends because they hold us back and don't encourage us to be the best we can be.

As I noted earlier, it's not cynical or self-serving to say that you have to choose your friends with care. Still, no matter how discerning you think you've been, you may let people into your life who will let you down. No matter how much love you give them, their own needs or weaknesses will trump that great gift. Like family members, friends do sometimes betray us. It's a truism, in fact, that no one can hurt you as deeply as a friend or loved one, because they know you best and know just where to stick the knife.

When friends betray us, it's not necessarily because they're "evil." A friend can let you down out of his own weakness, or because he simply can't see the world as you do, or out of fear or some other character flaw that makes it impossible for him to be there for you when you need him. We can all recall a situation from childhood when we were with a friend, our best buddy, walking home together after school, and turned a corner to find the sidewalk blocked by three big, mean eighth-graders on their bikes. They refused to let you pass, but you stood up to them, because you had your best buddy with you, watching your back. Then, when the big kid to your left grabbed your backpack and started to yank it off your shoulder, you turned to your friend . . . and saw him running away, abandoning you to your fate. He didn't do that because he was evil or because he didn't like you. He did it because he was weak and let his fear cancel out your friendship.

That's why in the military deserters are often executed. It's not because they felt overwhelming terror—every soldier does. It's because they ran away and abandoned their fellows.

In civilian life we don't execute our friends and colleagues who similarly desert us—much as we may want to. You are, however, justified in cutting that person out of your life, to prevent them from ever damaging you again in that way. As I noted above, my closest friends are the ones who've been tested, and proven faithful and trustworthy.

You can also learn from the experience when a friend lets you down. Analyze how you missed the signals and misled yourself about that person. What was it about you, and about him, that allowed you to make that mistake? You can become wiser about choosing your friends and colleagues.

Disappointments like that also bring us closer to those we know we can trust. In the end, learning to navigate your way through your relationships, the positive as well as the negative ones, and to remain steadfast and persevere in the pursuit of your own goals and happiness, is crucial to your success in life.

On the other hand, as you follow your path to personal happiness you may make decisions that you fear your friends or loved ones will see as a betrayal. There's a middle-class couple raising their kids in comfortable suburbia. One day the husband announces, "Honey, I know what I have to do to fulfill myself. We have to move to Central Africa. I'm going to do missionary work there." What if the wife doesn't want to give up everything they've worked for and move to Africa? And what about the kids? They're happy in school, they've got their friends—is this fair to them?

The first thing to remember is that **you owe it to your friends and loved ones, just as much as you owe it to yourself, to be the very best person you can be. You're not doing them any favors if you thwart your true desires and make yourself miserable.**

And if they're your true friends and truly love you, they'll stick with you.

That doesn't mean they won't question you when you make what seems to be a radical decision. In fact, if they love you, they *should* question you about it. I hope that if I woke up some morning and announced to Ann, "Honey, we're moving to Africa to become missionaries," she would challenge that decision. "Okay. Why Africa? What are you trying to achieve? How would you achieve it?" And so on.

It's a key to success to have people in your life who, because they love you and want the best for you and are not driven by self-interest, can help you figure out if in fact you're going down the right path. And once that's been determined, they support you in your quest.

Think how much better off Howard Hughes would have been had he surrounded himself with friends and loved ones like that, instead of isolating himself from all human contact in his "germ-free zone," where no amount of riches, fame, or success in the business world could make him happy.

YOUR COMMUNITY

In 1961, Americans cheered when President Kennedy told them, "Ask not what your country can do for you—ask what you can do for your country." Kennedy cherished the ideal that we should all look beyond ourselves, and beyond our immediate support group of family and friends, to become productive and contributing members of society. He firmly believed that each and every one of us owes a debt of service to the community. He well understood the cooperative power of humanity—that **we all derive enormous benefits if each of us is striving to do the best we can for our community as well as for ourselves and our immediate circle.**

Perhaps the most noble expression of this ideal of community service is the Peace Corps, founded in 1961 and directly inspired by a speech President Kennedy made to college students. The Peace Corps interprets the idea of community in its broadest sense—the community of mankind. In its forty-plus years, more than 170,000 Americans have volunteered their time and skills to

If a free society cannot help the many who are poor, it cannot save the few who are rich.

— JOHN F. KENNEDY

the service of others in 136 countries around the world. At the time of this writing, some 7,000 volunteers are at work in 70 poor and struggling nations, including 13 countries in Latin America. (And, by the way, the current director of the Peace Corps is the first Latin to run the organization, Gaddi H. Vasquez. He was born in Texas, the son of Mexican migrant workers.)

Something happened to this ideal of community service in the decades after the 1960s—the so-called Me Decade of the 1970s, the "greed is good" 1980s, and the go-go 1990s. Many people seemed to forget or ignore the debt we all owe to our community; it almost came to be seen as "uncool" and foolish to devote a part of one's life and energies to helping others.

But such selfishness and greed, as I've argued previously, are actually self-defeating. Your community forms a larger support group beyond your immediate circle of family and friends. On the most basic and obvious level, it provides tangible benefits and services to you and your loved ones, through your schools, hospitals, libraries, day-care centers, museums, theaters, parks, and countless other ways. If no one in your community actively participates in maintaining and improving those services, the quality of life for all of you will suffer.

While each of us must choose his or her own path in life, none of us lives in a social vacuum. You can in fact help yourself achieve your goals by helping others. Often the mutual benefits are direct and obvious. Recall Laurie, the photographer and single mother who decided that one way to reach her ultimate goal of becoming a filmmaker was to take small, immediate steps to revive her career in still photography. Working odd jobs, struggling every month to pay the rent and put food on the table for her ten-year-old daughter, she still made time to pursue her dream. She began to attend evening meetings of a professional photographers' association. Through this group, she volunteered to run an after-school photography class at a public middle school in her neighborhood. It was extremely difficult for her to make the time for this, but she found she loved working with the students and derived immense personal pleasure and a much-needed boost to her self-esteem from it.

But she also benefited in more direct ways. For one thing, the school had excellent darkroom facilities, and the grateful staff was more than willing to let her use the equipment to develop her own photographs along with the students'. So Laurie could build the professional portfolio she needed to find employment as a photographer—and do it for free. On top of that, the administrators of the school, which focused on gifted children, got to know Laurie's daughter and were so impressed with the youngster that they arranged for her to transfer there to take advantage of their accelerated learning program.

This is not an unusual story. You'd be amazed at how often that happens—how everyone benefits when you give back something to the community.

This story also demonstrates that you don't have to join the Peace Corps or become a missionary to get involved. **Wherever you live, and whatever time, skills, and talents you have to offer, there are many opportunities for you to give back something to your community.** Whether that's tutoring or mentoring young people in your field of expertise, participating in an organization like the Little League or the Scouts, becoming a Big Brother or Big Sister, lending a hand at your church's soup kitchen for the homeless, volunteering at your local hospital or senior center, joining the board of an arts organization, helping to organize fund-raisers for a charity—the opportunities are endless, and you can easily identify the ones that best match the time and skills you have to offer. I promise you that **contributing to your community will enrich your life with rewards that are far greater than money.**

REVIEW

- Those who are so driven to succeed that they'll sacrifice their friendships and their family life to achieve their goals are misguided and will never know true happiness.

- No one who has been truly successful and happy in life has done it alone.

- You owe it to your friends and loved ones, just as much as you owe it to yourself, to be the very best person you can be. You're not doing them any favors if you thwart your true desires and make yourself miserable.

- It's a key to success to have people in your life who, because they love you and want the best for you and are not driven by self-interest, can help you figure out if you're going down the right path. And who, once that's been determined, will support you in your quest.

- We all derive enormous benefits if each of us is striving to do the best we can for our community as well as for ourselves and our immediate circle. Wherever you live, and whatever time, skills, and talents you have to offer, there are many opportunities for you to give back something to your community. Contributing to your community will enrich your life with rewards that are far greater than money.

EXERCISE: What Can I Do to Help?

Each of us can contribute to our community, regardless of our occupation, background, education, skills, age, or any other factor. Remember, there really are no excuses for not striving to be the finest person you can be, and an integral part of that process is doing your best for those around you. Don't think you have nothing to contribute. You do, and it's easy to find those opportunities best suited to you.

If you're having trouble identifying what you can do for your community, try this simple exercise:

1. I have the following skills, talents, and/or expertise to offer:

   _____

   _____

2. I can reasonably devote this much time every week/month to this work:

   _____

   _____

3. The organization(s) in my immediate community where I think my time and talents would be most suited and useful is/are:

   _____

   _____

When you've answered those three simple questions, contact the organization(s) you've identified and offer to help. If a particular organization does not feel the need for your help at this time, they will surely know of others for you to contact.

Be Humble

Pride goeth before the fall.

—PROVERBS 6:18

We often see people—both those who achieve some measure of success and those who watch other people achieve—who clearly confuse the external trappings of success with true happiness and self-fulfillment. They may be rich and famous, they may have reached some pinnacle in their field, but they fail where it counts, as human beings. Those are the people who are most likely to let "success go to their heads," inevitably with negative results.

ARROGANCE AND HUBRIS

Human beings are social animals. We crave contact with others. It's a very rare human who can isolate himself from human contact and remain happy, or even sane. Psychologists have charted many sorts of neurotic and self-destructive behavior that stem from lack of human contact. Loneliness is a major cause of suicides.

As social beings, we seem to have an innate desire for the esteem and approval of others. In important ways our self-esteem is linked to how we are regarded by those around us. The psychologist Alfred Adler called this innate urge the "social interest." Like all desires, it can be expressed in a healthy way or in a neurotic, distorted way. Adler said it begins in infancy and early childhood, when the child craves the attention and later the approval of its mother. As the child grows and becomes more integrated in a wider community, he seeks the respect of others outside his immediate family circle. In healthy individuals, the social interest is part of what drives us to excel and be the best we can be. We enjoy earning the esteem of others when we are functioning at our best, both as an individual and as a member of our community.

Adler believed that some individuals have difficulty developing beyond the childish stage and integrating with society. In these people the urge to be the best they can be and earn the respect of those around them is distorted into a neurotic need to feel *superior* to those around them, to demand special treatment rather than earn respect—to "lord it over" others. These are precisely the type of people who mistake the outward trappings of success and happiness for the real thing. Usually they are trying to compensate for a lack of self-esteem and feelings of inferiority by attaining the external signs of success—wealth, fame, power, mindless acquisition, the ability to "boss people around"—and the false sense of superiority those things bring. Remember the billionaire in chapter 2 who seems so desperate to prove to everyone how successful he is by building the biggest mansion on the east coast of the United States—and in doing so, earning the disgust and disapproval of the very people he's hoping to impress. That building has nothing to do with being a "home." It's more like a giant, glaring symptom of this man's lack of self-respect.

One of the challenges you can face when you become a public success, as I did, is that it can distance you from others. Normal human interactions become strained. People begin to treat you differently and expect you to act differently. Some people are attracted to you not because of who you are but because of what you represent to them—money, power, fame, opportunity. You become a reflection of their desires and expectations. It's a deeply dehumanizing experience.

As I became successful, people began to treat me with a level of deference that I was not comfortable with. Suddenly, they wouldn't let me carry my own bags in and out of airports or hotels. I was a healthy man in his early thirties. I'd always carried my own bags. But now I had people around me all the time who'd snatch my bags out of my hands and carry them for me—as though I had somehow become too good to do it for myself.

My business meetings took on a new and weird tone as well. Increasingly, it came to be treated as a "perk" to meet me. People who worked for me became hesitant about simply coming to talk to me about issues—they would prepare a presentation. My interactions with them became very artificial. Journalists or potential investors or business partners would be ushered into my office as though they had been granted an audience with royalty. It became almost ceremonial. It was extremely disconcerting to relate to people that way. I felt that I was no longer Fernando Espuelas, entrepreneur, but playing the role of Fernando Espuelas, the media figure who was praised in *Time*.

In that kind of an environment, it can be easy to start believing your own hype, as the saying goes. The distorted image others have of you may become a distortion of your very personality. You may begin to think that you really are superior to other people, and that therefore you can mistreat and abuse them. You may come to believe in your own genius, your infallibility, your invulnerability—that you can "do no wrong."

Those are dangerous ideas to entertain. Arrogance is self-defeating. **Arrogance disconnects you from other people and from**

your own humanity. You forget that you didn't become a success on your own, but did so with the help and support of other people—your family and friends, mentors and advisers, partners and employees. As you isolate yourself from them, you cut yourself off from their useful ideas, their honest feedback, their criticism, and all the other information and advice they can bring. That's a sure way of setting yourself up for failure, for making a mistake or some error of judgment that could easily have been avoided if you'd listened to others and made yourself open to their honest opinions and advice.

The great dramatists of ancient Greece knew well the dangers of that sort of arrogance. We still use their word for overweening pride: hubris. In *Oedipus Rex*, Oedipus the king becomes so sure of his brilliance and wisdom that he refuses to hear the advice or warnings of others, even the famous soothsayer and prophet Tiresias. He stubbornly charges ahead on his own path, and in doing so brings ruin to himself and his family. By the end of the play he has caused his mother to commit suicide and has reduced himself to a blind beggar. In *The Bacchae*, King Pentheus is so arrogant that he openly disrespects Dionysius, one of the gods. Big mistake: Pentheus ends up literally ripped limb from limb by the god's followers.

In disconnecting yourself from others, you lose your own humanity. **Hubris and arrogance reduce you to something less than a human being: You become a caricature of yourself.**

No leader in modern history made himself more a caricature of arrogant power than Benito Mussolini, the fascist dictator of Italy and close ally of Adolf Hitler. Mussolini was a newspaper editor and political troublemaker who seized absolute power in 1922 as Italy's democratic institutions collapsed in the wake of World War I. Already extremely vain and egotistical, his absolute power vaulted him to absolute egomania. Some of the best-known film footage shows him on a balcony in Rome, luxuriating in the adulation of the cheering masses below. With his arms crossed over his barrel chest and his chin and lower lip thrust out in a look of psychopathic smugness, he appears more like a cartoon character than a real person, the epitome of imperious hubris.

Like the billionaire building a castle for himself, Mussolini reveled in symbolic visible displays of his superiority—what one critic dubbed "architectural brutalism." Mussolini loved to make a meeting with him seem like an audience with a godlike figure. In the vast palazzo in Rome from which he ruled, he had his desk set up at the end of a long, long hallway. If you were summoned to an appointment with him, you had to walk the entire length of this hallway while he sat haughtily behind his desk. By the time you finally got within speaking distance, you were almost guaranteed to feel properly cowed.

It is really no surprise that as soon as Mussolini's alliance with Hitler plunged Italy into demoralizing defeat, the same crowds who had cheered him in his glory days turned into bloodthirsty mobs. He was cast out of power in 1943, and had to throw himself on the mercy of his Nazi protectors. In 1945, when the Nazis could not shield him any longer, angry Italians caught up with Mussolini as he was trying to flee across the border into Switzerland. They summarily executed him, and hung him up by the heels in a public square, displaying his corpse the way fishermen might show off a dead shark. It's a sickening image, yet one can understand how millions of people whose lives were made miserable by this smug monster took satisfaction from his horrendous end.

History is replete with such examples. Mussolini's ally Adolf Hitler, who postured with grotesque self-satisfaction while orchestrating the obliteration of tens of millions of people, ended his days cowering in an underground bunker as his enemies reduced Germany to rubble and ashes. After he committed suicide, his body was flung in a ditch and burned like refuse. During the French Revolution, an entire generation of royals and nobles, who'd lived in supercilious grandeur while peasants starved, were guillotined before cheering crowds of those same peasants.

These stories also illustrate how **arrogance creates enemies.** Arrogance is an efficient factory for producing bad energy that spreads through all facets of your life. It's human nature to want to see an arrogant person fail. The term for it is *schadenfreude*, a German word which means rejoicing in someone else's misfortune. People naturally think how amusing, just, and satisfying it would be if that person were to experience a major downfall. Some people will take schadenfreude to the logical next step and try to *engineer* that fall—they see it as their mission to be the agent of that person's defeat.

In America today we tend not to behead fallen leaders or string up their corpses, but we still often rejoice in their downfall. The vain politician exposed in some scandal, the greedy Wall Streeter arrested for fraud, the egotistical celebrity or snotty socialite caught in some humiliating situation—they all evoke schadenfreude. As we noted earlier, there's a media industry focused intently on exposing successful people's foibles and weaknesses, and in doing so helping to bring about their just "comeuppance." Whole magazines and cable television channels seem to have been created for the sole purpose of cutting famous and successful people down to size and trumpeting scandals involving their marriages, sex lives, addictions, and so on.

We all know of successful figures who are abusive to their employees, rude to people they think they're better than, and so on. There's a saying that you should be careful how you treat other people on your way up the ladder to success, because you're going to meet them again on your way back down. When you falter or slip and could really use their help, they're going to remember how you mistreated them. **Arrogance is insecurity wrapped around power.** Arrogant people are showing their enemies that they're weak and vulnerable to attack.

One hallmark of arrogant people is that they believe their current level of success, whatever that is, is secure and permanent. They forget that all life is change and that no one can see into the future. They become convinced that because they're now enjoying some level of success, they will always be successful. They begin to think of themselves as invulnerable and infallible.

But as we all know, life *is* change. You don't know when the next seven-ton piano is going to drop on you from an apparently clear blue sky. **Arrogant and self-satisfied people are the *least* able to cope with change or challenges.** If they make a mistake or experience some failure, they take it much worse than they should, because they're not mentally prepared for it at all. Overweening pride creates a brittle, fragile ego. They've become so convinced of their own infallibility that when they make a mistake it's a crushing blow to their self-image and confidence. They've lost the flexibility and openness that helped them become successful in the first place, and that they need now to rebound from this current setback.

I know the fleeting nature of success all too well. When Star-Media was at its zenith, I could have easily succumbed to hubris and arrogance. The little company I had started with no more than a vision and a couple of maxed-out credit cards had blossomed into one of the world's largest Internet companies—and literally changed Latin American society. I was a world-famous entrepreneur in my early thirties, one of *Time*'s "Leaders for the Millennium." My fortune was worth half a billion dollars.

But everything changes. When the Internet, Wall Street, and the global economy all faltered at more or less the same time, I felt like another seven-ton piano was flattening me every day. The demise of StarMedia was a terrible blow to me. Had I believed my own hype, been convinced that I was a genius who could do no wrong, I don't know if I could have survived those cataclysmic events. I doubt if I would have had the resilience to accept those events for what they were—new challenges in my life, and new opportunities to create something even greater than I'd accomplished so far.

CYCLES OF HUMILITY

We know that life is a journey, filled with change and challenges, highs and lows. No stage in your life is permanent. Success follows failure, failure success. How does the Frank Sinatra song go? Riding high in April, shot down in May.

But it's not just that. Because life is a journey, it's critical to remember that no level of success is "the ultimate." You can never stop growing and striving to better yourself. You must never decide, "That's it. Being an assistant calculus professor at a community college is as good as I can manage. I'll never do better than this." Because you can *always* do better, always improve. No human being is complete and perfect. Only gods are perfect.

I've achieved what plenty of people would have called extraordinary success at several stages in my life. Had I simply decided, when I was doing so well at Ogilvy & Mather or AT&T, that I had accomplished all I was capable of, that there was no need to strive for more, I never would have created StarMedia and had the positive impact we had on so many lives. Had I decided that StarMedia was the best I could do, I wouldn't have created VOY.

The truth is, I don't know how much I can achieve. Neither do you. I hope I never get to a point where I think, "That's it. I've accomplished all I'm capable of." I hope I never stop challenging myself to grow and reach new heights. And I hope you don't, either.

Understanding that you'll never be perfect or achieve all you possibly can is the opposite of false pride and boastfulness: It's humility. Humility allows you to continue to grow, to learn, to keep expanding your horizons and face new challenges.

Humility also helps you to see and be okay with your fallibility and vulnerabilities. It lets you admit when you've made a mistake and learn from that error. No matter how successful you think you are, you never forget that you got there with the help and support of many other people—your loved ones, colleagues, mentors, and advisers. You remain open to their opinions, ideas, and criticism, and that's how you keep improving yourself and your performance in the world.

Humility helps to prevent confusing arrogance with self-confidence. As Adler pointed out, arrogance in fact betrays a *lack* of self-confidence. It is a sign of weakness. Humility and respect for others are signs of strength.

Remember the story of King Juan Carlos of Spain apologizing to a journalist for his lateness. Juan Carlos assumed power after Spain had been under the dictatorial rule of Generalissimo Francisco Franco for forty years. Juan Carlos had seen Franco's haughty, despotic leadership style (Franco had styled himself "El Caudillo," hauntingly similar to Mussolini's "Il Duce"), and when he assumed the throne upon Franco's death in 1975, he became a very different type of leader. He had the wisdom and humility to understand that a good king serves his people, not the other way around. He is unfailingly respectful of others, and earns their respect that way. Unlike Mussolini and Franco, he doesn't demand absolute obedience; he is, as strange as this might sound, a monarch who has overseen and carefully tended to the rebirth of democracy in his nation.

Humility was a hallmark of another kind of king—Elvis Presley. Elvis was (and is) one of the most famous people in the world. During his lifetime, he was certainly the biggest celebrity in the world. More than twenty-five years after his death he still has a vast global following, the most devoted of whom worship him like the cult of a secular god, with shrines and tales of miracles and pilgrimages to Graceland (the only home in the United States that receives more visitors is the White House).

For all that, Elvis remained humble all his life. He never forgot that he came from a shotgun shack in the boondocks of Mississippi, and that he was a truck driver when he made his first recording. He always knew that if it weren't for his fans he might still be driving that truck. Elvis showed his gratitude to his fans in many ways. He was unfailingly polite to everyone he met, addressing them, no matter who they were or what their station in life was, as "Sir" or "Miss" or "Ma'am." He never begrudged a fan an autograph. (Compare that to the Hollywood movie star who was recently chastised in the gossip columns for charging his fans $50 cash for an autograph.) He was unstintingly generous to his family, friends, and employees, and he gave an enormous amount of his wealth back to the community in gifts to numerous charities. It is estimated that Elvis made four billion dollars during his lifetime, and gave half of it away.

Others may admire arrogant people who grasp only the external trappings of success for what they accomplish, but they're never respected and may even be despised. They will certainly not be able to look to others for support or help when they most need it.

Those who show respect to others earn their respect in return.

How far you go in life depends on your being tender with the young, compassionate with the aged, sympathetic with the striving, and tolerant of the weak and strong. Because someday in life you will have been all of these.

— George Washington Carver

COMPASSION

When Germany was defeated in World War I, the victorious Allies met with German leaders in the palace of Versailles, outside Paris, to negotiate the terms of peace. Germany had started the war, which in its four years had unleashed apocalyptic levels of death and destruction throughout Europe, and the Allies were in no mood to be kind or compassionate to their defeated enemy. The Treaty of Versailles, which the Germans signed under protest in 1919, was supposedly designed to prevent Germany from ever being a military threat to its neighbors again. But the terms of the treaty were also quite obviously intended to punish the German people for the cataclysm they'd caused. To put it bluntly, the Allies wanted revenge.

And, despite the misgivings of many cooler heads, including Churchill, they got their revenge. Germany was not only reduced militarily, but was stripped of much land, forced into a humiliating admission of guilt, and committed to pay such enormous cash reparations to the Allies that the utter destruction of the nation's entire economy was assured. Germany was plunged into a brutal economic depression in the 1920s. This in turn caused complete political and social chaos.

This milieu of social decay, extreme poverty, and lingering national humiliation proved to be the perfect context for the rise of one of history's most brutal figures, Adolf Hitler. In seeking revenge against their enemy, the Allies had unwittingly sewn the seeds for World War II and all the horrors Hitler would unleash.

In 1945, when the Allies were again victorious over the Germans, Winston Churchill wisely advised that they heed the lesson of the Treaty of Versailles. He famously advocated, "In war, resolution; in defeat, defiance; in victory, magnanimity; in peace, goodwill." Instead of seeking revenge and creating new enemies, the Allies showed compassion toward the German people (while bringing their leaders to justice), and ensured that Germany would become a peaceful, productive member of European society.

Magnanimity is a form of compassion. Compassion has been described as the ability to see what the other sees, hear what the other hears, and feel what the other feels. Another term for this is empathy. Or love.

Compassion is a critical component of success. No matter what level of success you achieve, you must never allow it to convince you that you are superior to anyone else. You must always remember where you came from and who helped you achieve what you have. If your success somehow means someone else's failure—whether you beat someone at chess or win a lucrative landscaping contract to rebuild the town park—you must remember how it felt when *you* lost a competition, and be magnanimous about your victory.

If for no other reason, you must be compassionate out of enlightened self-interest. Never forget that though you may be successful today, tomorrow you may fail, or may feel the need to strive for even greater success. It's simply self-defeating to create enemies out of people who might help you when you need it next.

I know this lesson from personal experience. When StarMedia faltered and I decided to create VOY, I immediately found that many people who'd dealt with me in various ways during Star-Media's heyday were very willing and ready to help and support my new efforts. My behavior during StarMedia's successful years had created friends and supporters, not enemies. Luckily, I had never allowed success to go to my head. I never forgot that I had started out a penniless immigrant. Remembering who you really are and where you come from is an excellent way to prevent yourself from believing your own hype, mistreating others, and creating enemies.

REVIEW

- Do not let success go to your head. Arrogance disconnects you from other people and from your own humanity. Hubris and arrogance reduce you to something less than a human being: You become a caricature of yourself.

- Arrogance creates enemies. It's human nature to want to see an arrogant person fail.

- Arrogance is insecurity wrapped around power. Arrogant people are showing their enemies that they're weak and vulnerable to attack.

- Arrogant and self-satisfied people are the least able to cope with change or challenges.

- Like trust and honesty, true respect is earned by those who show respect to others.

EXERCISE: Arrogance and Humility

It's human nature that we can spot arrogance in other people more easily than in ourselves. Answer True or False to the following questions, as honestly as you can. Then show your answers to a friend or loved one who knows you well and whose opinion you trust. How accurate will they think your answers are?

1. I can't really feel good about anything I accomplish unless others notice and praise me for it.

2. I feel a constant need to "prove" myself to others.

3. I thrive on competition, because I enjoy the feeling of being better than everyone else.

4. Whenever I compete, winning is everything, and I try to win at all costs.

5. When I am competing with others, I see them as the enemy.

6. If I lose a competition, I'm good about accepting the results gracefully and congratulating the winner for his achievement.

7. When I win a competition, I'm gracious about it and try to empathize with those who lost.

8. When I win a competition, what I like best is knowing that I have beaten the others.

9. When I am successful in an endeavor, I like to brag and boast about it. I don't worry about how that may make others feel. If they don't like it, they're just "sore losers."

10. When I achieve success in an endeavor, I'm good about giving credit to everyone who helped and supported me.

11. When I see others achieve success, I'm often envious and think they don't deserve it.

12. When I see others achieve success, I often hope for their downfall.

13. When I make a mistake, I'm good about admitting it and accepting responsibility for it.

(continued)

14. When I make a mistake, I'm good about hearing constructive criticism and advice.

15. I relish the feeling that I have power and control over others.

16. When I'm in a position of power or leadership, the success of the whole team is as important to me as my personal success.

17. When I'm in a position of power, I'm often paranoid that those below me envy me and are plotting against me.

Your Journey

Begins Now

*O*nce, after a rough week, I sighed to an acquaintance and said, "Life can sure be complicated."

"Yes," she said, "life is hell. But there's a better place after."

Of course, my ears pricked up. In the first place, if you really believe life is hell, there's a problem with how you're living. And if your life is hell *and you're not doing anything about that*, you're doing yourself, and the rest of the world, a giant disservice.

I explained to her my philosophy, described in chapter 1, of the dangers of deferring happiness to some far-off time. I spoke about the importance of assuming that every day is a precious commodity that must be taken advantage of, and that you owe it to yourself, as well as to the rest of the community, to try to be your best and do your best every day of your life.

"I don't know what happens after we're dead," I said to her. "But even if there is 'a better place after,' don't you owe it to yourself to have done whatever you could to make *this* world better while you were living in it?"

"But how do you know what to do?" she replied. "What if you don't even know what it is you want to do? I just know I'm not happy. But what else is out there for me? How do I get there?"

I wrote this book for her. And for anyone else who finds himself or herself in a similar state. Because your life should not be hell. And if that's the way you feel, you can and should change your life.

It is my hope that through reading this book you have come to understand that you *can* achieve happiness and success. That you can seek happiness right now, today, instead of putting off your joy to some future date. And that you owe it to yourself, to your loved ones, and to your community to be striving for that happiness every single day of your life.

As you begin your journey, it's important to understand that success and happiness are not some distant, static, passive state you may attain at some point and then stop striving. Happiness is not a permanent vacation from life. The point is the journey itself, not the destination. Every day brings with it opportunities to be happy and successful. Happiness is growth, change, and progress. No life is ever complete, and no one is perfect.

Your life, your talents, your dreams, who you are, and what you can accomplish in this world—these all add up to a precious gift. I hope this book has inspired you in some way to make the best use of that gift you can, for yourself and for those around you. If you accept the challenge to be the finest person you can be, I promise that you will find the journey filled with excitement, joy, and deeply satisfying rewards.

The time is now.

VOY, *I go.*

ABOUT THE AUTHOR

Fernando Espuelas is the founder of VOY, a company with operations in television, film, publishing, music, and the Internet. VOY's core message is that self-actualization and optimism are the keys to success and personal fulfillment.

With a history of building globally recognized brands and as a strong advocate of empowering and connecting Latins, Espuelas cofounded and was formerly chairman and CEO of StarMedia Network, a pioneering Internet media company for Spanish- and Portuguese-speaking audiences worldwide. At StarMedia, he established a network that has broken national barriers to become the most recognized Internet brand in Latin America, serving 25 million people worldwide.

Espuelas's visionary leadership has earned him international recognition. *Time* magazine honored him as one of the "Leaders for the Millennium," and he was recognized as a "2000 All-Star" business leader by *Crain's New York Business*. The World Economic Forum includes him among its elite "Global Leaders of Tomorrow," and he was a recipient of *Latin Trade* Magazine's prestigious Bravo Award. He lives in New York.

For more information, go to **www.voygroup.com**.